# WYGDN What You Gonna Do Now

Jacques Chambers

# TABLE OF CONTENTS

# CHAPTER 1

Alex Parker sat at his desk, the steady hum of the office, a comforting white noise that had become as familiar as his own heartbeat. The screen in front of him displayed rows of financial data, each number a small piece of a puzzle that had once excited him but now felt more like a monotonous chore. He glanced at the clock, noting it was nearly noon, and considered whether he should grab a coffee or push through until lunch.

Before he could decide, his phone buzzed on the desk. A message from his boss, David Whitmore, lit up the screen:

Can you come to my office?

Alex felt a twinge of unease. The message was brief, devoid of the usual pleasantries that David, a man who prided himself on his approachability, typically included. Shaking off the feeling, Alex stood, smoothing his tie as he walked across the open-plan office. His colleagues barely looked up, each absorbed in their own tasks, their faces washed in the blue glow of computer monitors.

David's office was at the far end of the floor, a glass-enclosed space that symbolized the power and responsibility Alex had once aspired to. He knocked lightly on the door and entered at David's beckon.

"Alex, have a seat," David said, gesturing to the chair across from his desk. The tone in his voice was calm but heavy, like a storm cloud looming on the horizon.

Alex sat down, trying to ignore the way his palms suddenly felt damp against his thighs. He noticed the papers on David's desk, neatly stacked but with one sheet slightly askew, like something had been quickly shuffled out of sight.

"David, what's this about?" Alex asked, attempting to keep his tone light.

David sighed, leaning back in his chair. "I won't beat around the bush, Alex. You've been a valuable member of the team, but the company's going through some changes. Restructuring, they're calling it. And unfortunately… we have to let you go."

For a moment, the words didn't register. They hung in the air, foreign and impossible. Alex stared at David, searching his face for some sign that this was a mistake, a misunderstanding. But David's expression was somber, his eyes full of an apology that offered no solace.

"Let me go?" Alex repeated, the words tasting bitter on his tongue. "David, I've been with the company for eight years. My team just hit every target for the quarter. How… how does this make any sense?"

David sighed again, this time with a touch of weariness. "I know, Alex. Believe me, I fought for you, but the decisions are coming from above. They're cutting costs, and middle management is the first to go. It's not about your performance; it's just business."

It's just business. The phrase echoed in Alex's mind, a cold dismissal of the years he had poured into his work, the late nights, the missed family dinners. He felt a knot tighten in his chest, anger and disbelief warring within him.

"What about my severance?" Alex asked, his voice strained. "There's a severance package, right?"

David nodded, pushing a folder across the desk. "It's all in here. Three months' pay, health benefits for six months, and we'll provide a reference, of course. I'm truly sorry, Alex. If there was anything more I could do…"

Alex didn't respond. He picked up the folder, the weight of it feeling heavier than it should. He stood, forcing himself to meet David's eyes.

"I appreciate everything you've done, David," he said, the words hollow and automatic. "But I need to get home. I need to… figure things out."

David nodded, rising from his chair as well. "Take care, Alex. If you need anything—anything at all—don't hesitate to reach out."

Alex barely registered the words as he left the office, walking past rows of desks where his colleagues continued their work, unaware of the upheaval that had just rocked his world. The elevator ride down felt interminable, each floor passing in a blur of numbers that no longer held any meaning.

When the doors finally opened to the lobby, Alex stepped out into the midday sun, the warmth of it a stark contrast to the cold numbness spreading through his chest. He walked to his car, his steps heavy, his mind a whirlwind of thoughts and fears. How would he tell Lisa? What would they do about the mortgage? How had everything gone so wrong, so quickly? As he drove home, the familiar route felt strange, as if the world had shifted slightly, leaving everything off-kilter. The house came into view—a modest two-story with a well-tended lawn that he and Lisa had bought when Emma was born, a symbol of the life they were building together.

But now, as Alex pulled into the driveway, the house felt like a burden, a looming reminder of responsibilities he wasn't sure he could meet anymore. He sat in the car for a moment, staring at the front door, dreading the conversation that awaited him inside. With a deep breath, Alex finally got out of the car, his legs feeling unsteady as he walked to the door. He pushed it open and stepped into the quiet of the house, the familiar scent of Lisa's cooking wafting from the kitchen. For a brief moment, he considered not telling her, pretending everything was fine just for a little longer. But the folder in his hand was a cold, hard reality he couldn't ignore. Alex took another deep breath, preparing himself for the difficult conversation ahead.

Alex stood in the foyer, the familiar sounds of home washing over him like a wave that threatened to pull him under. The soft clatter of pots and pans came from the kitchen, and the distant murmur of the television drifted from the living room where Emma was likely doing her homework with the TV on low, just as she did every day after school. It was all so ordinary, and yet today it felt surreal, as if he was watching his life through a pane of glass, disconnected from the reality of it.

He placed his keys on the table by the door, the sound of them hitting the wood unusually loud in the quiet of the house. His hand hovered over the folder for a moment before he dropped it next to the keys, its presence a weight that pressed on him from all sides.

"Alex, is that you?" Lisa's voice called from the kitchen, pulling him back to the present.

He took a deep breath and forced himself to move forward, to cross the threshold into the room where Lisa was busy stirring something on the stove. She looked up as he entered, a small, welcoming smile on her face. For a moment, Alex just stood there, taking in the sight of her—her dark hair pulled back into a ponytail, her face lightly flushed from the heat of the stove, the scent of garlic and onions filling the air. It was a snapshot of normalcy, of the life they had built together, and it almost brought tears to his eyes.

"Dinner will be ready in about twenty minutes," Lisa said, turning back to the stove. "How was your day?"

It was such a simple question, and yet Alex felt his chest tighten as he struggled to find the words. How was his day? His day had been the beginning of the end, a seismic shift that had cracked the foundation of everything he thought was secure.

"It was a day, that's for sure," he finally said, his voice strained.

Lisa paused, glancing at him over her shoulder. "That doesn't sound good. What happened?"

Alex hesitated, the words sticking in his throat. He didn't want to see the worry in her eyes, didn't want to burden her with the fear that was gnawing at him. But there was no avoiding it. She deserved to know.

"Lisa, I... I lost my job today."

The spoon in Lisa's hand clattered against the pot as she turned to face him fully, her expression a mixture of surprise and concern. "What? What do you mean? Why?"

"They're calling it restructuring," Alex said, trying to keep his voice steady. "Cost-cutting measures. I was just... I was just on the list."

For a moment, there was only silence between them, the words hanging heavy in the air. Then, Lisa stepped forward, her hands reaching out to grasp his. "Alex, I'm so sorry. I know how much that job meant to you."

He nodded, the lump in his throat growing larger. "It's not just the job, Lisa. It's everything—the mortgage, Emma's college fund, our future... I don't know what we're going to do."

"We'll figure it out," Lisa said, her voice firm and reassuring. "We always do. We'll cut back on expenses, dip into savings if we have to. And you'll find another job. It's not the end of the world."

But Alex couldn't shake the feeling that it was the end of the world, at least the world he had known. He appreciated Lisa's optimism, her unwavering belief that things would work out, but right now, all he could see were the cracks forming in the life they had built, each one threatening to widen into a chasm that could swallow them whole.

He squeezed her hands, drawing strength from her even as his mind raced with fears and uncertainties. "I hope you're right," he said quietly, though he didn't feel the conviction behind his words.

Lisa gave him a small smile, the kind that was meant to reassure but didn't quite reach her eyes. "I know I am. Why don't you go relax for a bit? Dinner's almost ready, and then we can talk about this more after Emma goes to bed."

Alex nodded, grateful for the momentary reprieve. He knew they needed to talk about it, needed to plan their next steps, but he wasn't ready to face that just yet. He turned to leave the kitchen, but something in Lisa's expression made him pause. There was a shadow there, a flicker of something that looked almost like guilt, but before he could question it, she turned back to the stove, resuming her work with a forced cheerfulness that only deepened his unease. He left the kitchen and walked into the living room, where Emma was sprawled on the couch with her textbooks, her long hair falling over her face as she concentrated on her work. She looked up as he entered, giving him a quick smile before returning to her homework. The sight of her, so focused and innocent, brought a fresh wave of emotion crashing over him. He had always wanted to provide the best for her, to give her a life full of opportunities. But now, with his job gone, he didn't know how he was going to keep that promise.

Alex sat down in his favorite armchair, the one that was perfectly broken in from years of use, and stared out the window at the fading light of the evening. The neighborhood was quiet, the kind of suburban peace he had once taken for granted. But now, with his mind racing and his heart heavy, that peace felt fragile, like it could shatter at any moment. He closed his eyes, trying to steady his breathing, trying to push back the rising tide of panic that threatened to overwhelm him. But no matter how hard he tried, the reality of his situation pressed in on him from all sides, a relentless reminder that the life he had known was slipping through his fingers, and he had no idea how to stop it.

Dinner was a quiet affair, despite Lisa's attempts to keep the conversation light. Alex pushed the food around his plate, nodding at the appropriate moments when Lisa or Emma spoke, but his thoughts were elsewhere, tangled in a web of fear and uncertainty.

As the meal wrapped up, the doorbell rang, pulling Alex out of his reverie. He glanced at Lisa, who gave him a knowing smile. "That'll be Mom and Dad," she said, getting up to answer the door.

Alex had forgotten about the family dinner they'd planned for tonight. Lisa's parents came over almost every week for a casual meal, a tradition that had started after Emma was born. Normally, Alex looked forward to these evenings—his in-laws were easygoing, their conversation filled with the kind of everyday banter that kept the world spinning on an even keel. But tonight, the thought of sitting through a meal, pretending everything was fine, felt like an impossible task.

"Emma, help me clear the table before your grandparents come in," Lisa called from the foyer. Emma got up without complaint, her teenage sulkiness temporarily replaced with a sense of duty. Alex watched her gather the plates, feeling a stab of guilt. She had no idea how close they were to losing everything they had worked for.

He forced himself to get up and carry the glasses to the kitchen, trying to push down the rising panic. He wasn't ready to tell Lisa's parents about the layoff. He wasn't ready to tell anyone. He needed time to figure things out, to come up with a plan. The last thing he wanted was for them to worry, to see him as a failure.

"Alex, you okay?" Lisa's mother, Margaret, asked as she entered the kitchen, her sharp eyes catching the tension in his posture.

Alex plastered on a smile, the kind he'd perfected for office meetings where showing vulnerability was not an option. "Yeah, just a long day at work," he said, trying to keep his tone casual.

Margaret nodded, satisfied for the moment, and began unpacking the dessert she'd brought—a homemade apple pie that filled the kitchen with a comforting aroma. "Well, you're in for a treat. I made your favorite."

Alex mumbled a word of thanks, focusing on stacking the dishes in the sink. The normalcy of the routine was a strange comfort, even though it felt like a flimsy facade that could collapse at any moment. He felt like an actor in a play, following the script even as his mind screamed that everything was falling apart behind the scenes.

They all gathered around the dining room table again, the remnants of dinner pushed aside to make room for pie and coffee. The conversation flowed easily, Lisa's parents chatting about their day, Emma talking about a school project, Lisa chiming in with updates from work. Alex nodded along, contributing when necessary, but his mind was elsewhere, running through the numbers in his head, calculating how long their savings would last, wondering how many months he could keep up appearances before everything came crashing down.

As the evening wore on, Alex found himself retreating into silence, content to let the others carry the conversation. He listened to the sound of their voices, the clink of forks against plates, the hum of the dishwasher in the background. It all felt so normal, so achingly normal, that for a brief moment, he could almost pretend that nothing had changed.

But then Margaret asked about work, and the illusion shattered.

"So, how's everything going at the office, Alex? Still keeping busy?" she asked, her tone light and conversational.

Alex felt a flash of panic, his mind scrambling for a response that wouldn't give away the truth. "Yeah, still busy," he said, his voice sounding too bright, too forced. "Same old, same old."

Lisa glanced at him, her brow furrowing slightly, but she didn't say anything. Her father, Frank, nodded, oblivious to the tension simmering beneath the surface.

"Good to hear. Job security is everything these days."

Job security. The words echoed in Alex's mind, a bitter reminder of what he had lost. He forced a smile, hoping it didn't look as strained as it felt.

"Absolutely," he said, taking a long sip of his coffee to avoid saying anything more.

The conversation moved on, but Alex barely heard it. He focused on maintaining his mask, on keeping up the charade, even as guilt gnawed at him from the inside. He knew he couldn't keep this up forever, knew that eventually, the truth would have to come out. But not tonight. Tonight, he just needed to get through the evening, to hold onto this small semblance of normalcy for as long as he could.

Finally, the evening began to wind down. Emma hugged her grandparents goodnight, and Lisa walked them to the door, exchanging the usual pleasantries about getting together again soon. Alex stayed in the kitchen, cleaning up the last of the dishes, his hands moving on autopilot as his mind raced.

When Lisa returned, she gave him a long, searching look. "You sure you're okay?" she asked quietly, her voice tinged with concern.

Alex nodded, not trusting himself to speak. He turned off the tap, drying his hands with a dish towel. "Just tired," he said, avoiding her gaze.

Lisa watched him for a moment longer, then nodded. "Okay. Let's get some rest, then."

They went upstairs in silence, the weight of the day pressing down on them both. As Alex lay in bed that night, staring up at the ceiling, he felt the walls closing in, the darkness of the room mirroring the darkness in his mind. He knew he couldn't keep the truth hidden forever. But for tonight, he could pretend. Pretend that everything was still okay, that he was still the provider, the protector, the man who had it all together.

But deep down, he knew it was only a matter of time before the truth would come crashing down, and he would have to face the question that loomed over him like a dark cloud.

What on Earth are you gonna do now, Alex?

# CHAPTER 2

It had been just over six months since he was laid off, and Alex had yet to tell anyone beyond Lisa. He couldn't bring himself to admit the truth to his friends or family, and Lisa, for her part, hadn't pushed him. She seemed to understand that he needed time to process, to come to terms with what had happened. But the weight of the secret was growing heavier each day, a constant presence that followed him everywhere. There was no office to go to in the morning, so, instead of driving to the office, he wandered aimlessly, sitting in coffee shops, or driving around the city, trying to figure out his next move. The days blurred together, each one a reminder of the stability he'd lost and the uncertainty that now defined his life.

One afternoon, after another fruitless job search, Alex found himself sitting in his car outside a park. He watched as children played on the swings, their laughter ringing out across the playground. Parents sat on benches, chatting or watching their kids with fond smiles. It was a scene of innocence and simplicity, a world that seemed untouched by the kind of worries that now plagued him. He sighed, leaning back in his seat and closing his eyes. He could feel the beginnings of a headache, a dull throb at the base of his skull. The stress was beginning to take its toll, not just on his mind but on his body as well. His thoughts drifted to Lisa, wondering how she was handling it all. She had been distant lately, her usual warmth replaced with a kind of cool efficiency. She did what needed to be done, but there was a distance between them that hadn't been there before.

It's just the stress, Alex told himself. She's worried too. She's probably just trying to hold it together for Emma's sake.

But even as he tried to convince himself, a small voice in the back of his mind whispered that something was wrong. Lisa had always been his rock, the one who kept everything steady even when the world seemed to be falling apart. But now, she felt like a stranger, her thoughts and emotions hidden behind a wall he couldn't breach.

Alex opened his eyes and glanced at the dashboard clock. It was late afternoon, and he knew he couldn't stay out much longer without raising suspicion. With a heavy sigh, he started the car and headed home, bracing himself for another evening of pretending everything was fine.

When he arrived, the house was quiet. Emma was at a friend's house, and Lisa's car was in the driveway, but she wasn't in the kitchen or living room. Alex set his briefcase down and headed upstairs, thinking she might be resting. As he approached their bedroom, he noticed the door was slightly ajar, and he could hear Lisa's voice, low and urgent.

He stopped, his hand hovering over the door handle, a sense of unease creeping over him. Something about the tone of her voice made his skin prickle. He listened, the words muffled but distinct enough to catch the general gist of the conversation.

"…I don't know how much longer I can keep this up," Lisa was saying, her voice strained. "He's going to find out eventually, and when he does…"

There was a pause, followed by a murmur of words that Alex couldn't quite make out. He felt a cold knot form in the pit of his stomach as he realized she was on the phone with someone. The low, masculine tones on the other end of the line sent a shiver down his spine.

"No, I haven't told him yet," Lisa continued, her voice tinged with frustration. "I can't just drop this on him out of nowhere. He's already dealing with so much."

The knot tightened, his mind racing as he tried to make sense of what he was hearing. Who was she talking to? What hadn't she told him?

"I know, I know," Lisa said, her voice dropping to a whisper. "I'll handle it, okay? Just… give me a little more time."

Alex felt his breath catch in his throat. His hand, still hovering over the door, slowly curled into a fist. His pulse pounded in his ears, drowning out the rest of the conversation. He couldn't stand there any longer, couldn't listen to whatever else she might say.

He pushed the door open, his heart hammering in his chest. Lisa was sitting on the edge of the bed, her back to him, phone pressed to her ear. She didn't hear him enter, too absorbed in her conversation.

"Lisa?" Alex's voice was sharp, cutting through the air like a knife.

Lisa jumped, nearly dropping the phone. She spun around, her eyes wide with shock. For a moment, neither of them moved, the silence between them thick and heavy.

"Who are you talking to?" Alex asked, his voice low and controlled, though it took every ounce of willpower to keep it that way.

Lisa's hand trembled as she slowly lowered the phone. "Alex… it's not what you think."

He stepped closer, his gaze hardening. "Then what is it? Because from where I'm standing, it sounds like you've been keeping something from me."

Lisa swallowed hard, her eyes flicking away from his. "I was going to tell you… I just didn't know how."

"Tell me what?" Alex's voice rose, the control he'd been clinging to slipping away. "Who were you talking to?"

Lisa hesitated, her eyes filled with something Alex couldn't quite decipher—guilt, fear, maybe both. "It's… it's not what you think," she repeated weakly.

The frustration, the fear, the uncertainty—it all exploded in that moment, crashing over Alex like a tidal wave. "For God's sake, Lisa, just tell me the truth! I'm already hanging by a thread here—I can't take any more lies!"

Lisa flinched at his outburst, but then something seemed to harden in her gaze. She stood up, clutching the phone tightly. "You want the truth?" she said, her voice shaking. "Fine. I've been talking to someone. But it's not because I don't love you. It's because I'm scared, Alex. I'm scared of what's happening to us, of what's going to happen if we keep going like this."

Alex stared at her, his anger momentarily stunned into silence by her words. "What do you mean?" he asked, his voice softer now, but no less urgent.

Lisa took a deep breath, as if steeling herself for what she was about to say. "I've been seeing someone, Alex. Someone from work. It started a few months ago, before all of this happened. I didn't plan it—it just… it just happened. And now, with everything that's going on, I didn't know how to end it, how to tell you."

The words hit Alex like a physical blow, knocking the breath from his lungs. For a moment, he just stood there, staring at her as the reality of what she'd said sank in. The room seemed to tilt, the walls closing in as a wave of nausea rose in his throat.

"You… you've been seeing someone?" he echoed, his voice barely a whisper.

Lisa's eyes filled with tears as she nodded, her lips trembling. "I'm so sorry, Alex. I didn't mean for it to happen. I never wanted to hurt you."

The pain in her voice was real, but it did nothing to quell the storm of emotions raging inside him. Betrayal, anger, disbelief—they all swirled together, threatening to consume him. The woman he'd loved, the woman he'd trusted, had been seeing someone else behind his back, all while he was fighting to keep their lives from falling apart.

He took a step back, his hands clenching into fists at his sides. "How long?" he demanded, his voice rough.

"About six months," Lisa admitted, her voice barely audible. "But it's over, Alex. I ended it. I'm so sorry."

"Six months," Alex repeated, the words like acid on his tongue. "Six months, and you didn't think to tell me? You didn't think I deserved to know?"

Lisa shook her head, tears streaming down her cheeks. "I didn't want to make things worse. I didn't want to destroy everything we have."

"Well, congratulations," Alex snapped, his anger boiling over. "You did a hell of a job with that."

He turned away, unable to look at her any longer, his mind reeling. This was too much. He had already lost his job, his sense of security, and now, the one person he thought he could rely on had betrayed him in the worst possible way.

"Alex, please," Lisa sobbed, reaching out to him. "I know I messed up, but I love you. I want to fix this. I want us to be okay again."

But Alex couldn't hear her through the roar of his own emotions. He felt like he was drowning, the ground beneath his feet giving way as everything he thought he knew crumbled around him. He needed to get out, needed to clear his head, to escape the suffocating weight of it all.

Without another word, he stormed out of the room, ignoring Lisa's desperate pleas. He grabbed his keys and jacket, his movements jerky and frantic, and then he was out the door, slamming it behind him with a finality that echoed through the house.

The cool evening air hit Alex like a shock as he stepped outside, but it did little to calm the storm raging inside him. He walked briskly down the street, not knowing where he was going, only that he needed to keep moving. He needed to outrun the pain, the anger, and the overwhelming sense of betrayal that threatened to suffocate him.

The sun was setting, casting a golden light over the quiet suburban neighborhood, but Alex barely noticed. His thoughts were a chaotic swirl of emotions, each one more painful than the last. How could this have happened? How could Lisa, the woman he had loved and trusted for years, betray him like this?

He found himself at the park, the same one he had visited earlier that day. The playground was empty now, the children and parents gone home for the night. Alex sank onto a bench, his head in his hands as the weight of everything came crashing down on him.

He had lost his job, his sense of security, and now, the one person he thought he could rely on had shattered his heart. It felt like the universe was conspiring against him, tearing apart everything he had worked so hard to build. For the first time in a long while, Alex felt utterly and completely alone. The loneliness gnawed at him, deepening the void inside his chest. He had always been a man of faith, had always believed that there was a plan, a purpose to everything. But now, as he sat there in the gathering darkness, that belief seemed hollow, almost laughable.

Where are You now? Alex thought bitterly, his eyes lifting to the sky. Where are You when everything I've worked for is being taken away from me?

The sky above was vast and indifferent, the first stars beginning to twinkle in the fading light. Alex stared at them, his heart heavy with the weight of his doubts. He had prayed, had done everything he was supposed to do, and yet, here he was—jobless, betrayed, and lost.

*Why?* The question echoed in his mind, a relentless whisper that wouldn't go away. *Why is this happening to me? What did I do to deserve this?*

But there was no answer, only the distant hum of traffic and the rustling of leaves in the breeze. The silence was deafening, a void that seemed to swallow him whole. For the first time in his life, Alex felt like God had abandoned him, had turned His back when Alex needed Him the most.

The thought sent a fresh wave of pain through him, sharp and cutting. He had always taken comfort in his faith, had always believed that God was with him, guiding him through the trials of life. But now, that comfort was gone, replaced by a cold, empty void that left him questioning everything he had ever believed. *If God is real, if He cares, then why is this happening?* The thought was blasphemous, but Alex couldn't stop it from taking root in his mind. It was a seed of doubt, one that threatened to grow and consume him if he let it.

He sat there for a long time, his thoughts a dark and tangled mess. The night grew darker, the air cooler, but still, Alex didn't move. He was lost, adrift in a sea of uncertainty, with no anchor to hold onto, no light to guide him out of the darkness.

The days that followed were some of the darkest of Alex's life. He barely spoke to Lisa, the pain of her betrayal too fresh, too raw to confront. They moved around each other like ghosts, careful not to touch, not to speak, each wrapped in their own cocoon of misery. Alex spent most of his time in a daze, going through the motions of life but feeling nothing. He avoided his friends, avoided church, and avoided anything that might force him to confront the reality of his situation. He was a shell of the man he used to be, hollowed out by pain and doubt. Every night, he found himself lying awake, staring at the ceiling, his mind racing with questions he couldn't answer. The words became a mantra, a constant refrain in the back of his mind. Why had this happened? Why had God allowed it? Why had He turned His back on Alex when he needed Him the most?

The questions gnawed at him, eroding what little faith he had left. He wanted to believe that there was a reason for all of this, that somehow, it was all part of a greater plan. But the more he tried to hold onto that belief, the more it slipped through his fingers, leaving him feeling empty and abandoned.

One Sunday morning, about two weeks after he had discovered Lisa's affair, Alex found himself sitting in the living room, staring blankly at the television. Lisa was upstairs, probably getting ready to go to church. She had asked him to come with her, but he had refused. The thought of sitting in that pew, of pretending everything was fine when it was anything but, was too much to bear. The house was quiet, save for the low hum of the TV. Alex wasn't really watching, his mind too consumed with his own thoughts to pay attention. The screen flickered, the images a blur as his eyes drifted to the coffee table, where his Bible sat, untouched. For a long moment, Alex just stared at it, a feeling of dread settling in his chest. He hadn't opened it in weeks, hadn't prayed, hadn't even thought about God except in moments of anger and bitterness. The book that had once brought him so much comfort now felt like a stranger, something foreign and unapproachable.

"What's the point?" He asked nobody.

It was a bitter question but it rang true in his mind. What was the point of praying, of reading those words, when they had done nothing to stop his life from falling apart? What was the point of faith when it didn't protect him from the worst kinds of pain?

And yet, as much as he tried to push those thoughts away, there was something else there, a small, persistent whisper that refused to be silenced. It was the voice of his mother, long gone now, but her words still echoed in his mind.

"God doesn't promise that life will be easy, Alex," she had told him once, when he was a boy, struggling with the death of his first pet. "But He does promise that He will be with you, no matter what."

No matter what.

The words resonated in his mind, a faint glimmer of light in the darkness that had engulfed him. He didn't want to listen, didn't want to believe that there was still hope, still something worth holding onto. But the whisper grew louder, more insistent, until he couldn't ignore it any longer. With a deep sigh, Alex reached out and picked up the Bible. It felt heavy in his hands, the weight of it both familiar and foreign. For a moment, he just held it, his heart pounding in his chest. He didn't know what he was looking for, didn't know if he would find anything that could help him. But he had to try. He had to believe that there was still something worth believing in.

Slowly, he opened the book, flipping through the pages until he came to the Psalms. He had always found comfort in them, the words of David speaking to him in times of trouble. He began to read, his eyes skimming over the familiar verses, but this time, they felt different, more personal.

"The Lord is my shepherd; I shall not want. He maketh me to lie down in green pastures: He leadeth me beside the still waters. He restoreth my soul..."

The words washed over him, a balm to his wounded spirit. He read on, the verses flowing through him, filling the emptiness inside him with something warm, something comforting. He had read these words a hundred times before, but now, in this moment, they took on a new meaning, a new significance. For the first time in weeks, Alex felt a flicker of hope, a small, fragile thing, but it was there, growing stronger with each word he read. It was as if God was speaking to him directly, reminding him that he wasn't alone, that even in his darkest moments, there was still light, still a path forward. Tears filled Alex's eyes as he closed the Bible, holding it to his chest. He had been so angry, so lost in his own pain, that he had forgotten what it meant to have faith, to trust that there was a plan, even if he couldn't see it. But now, sitting there in the quiet of his living room, he felt something shift inside him. It was small, barely noticeable, but it was there—a tiny seed of faith, of hope, that had taken root.

It wasn't much, but it was enough. And for the first time in a long while, Alex allowed himself to believe that maybe, just maybe, he could find his way back to the light.

In the days that followed, Alex began to rebuild his faith, slowly and tentatively, like a man learning to walk again after a long illness. It wasn't easy, and there were times when the doubts still crept in, whispering that it was all pointless, that nothing could change the pain he was feeling. But each time those thoughts surfaced, Alex returned to the Bible, to prayer, to the small, simple rituals that had once brought him so much comfort.

He started attending church again, though it was hard at first. The first Sunday back, he sat in the back row, feeling like an outsider in a place that had once been a second home. But as the weeks went by, he began to feel more at ease, the familiar hymns and sermons wrapping around him like a warm blanket.

Pastor John noticed his return and reached out, offering a listening ear, but Alex wasn't ready to talk about everything just yet. It was enough that he was there, that he was starting to find his way back. The pain of Lisa's betrayal was still there, a constant ache in his chest, but it didn't consume him the way it had before. He was learning to let go, to forgive, not just Lisa, but himself as well. Alex spent more time in prayer, though his prayers were different now. They weren't the desperate, pleading cries he had once uttered, but quieter, more introspective. He prayed for strength, for guidance, for the wisdom to understand why things had happened the way they had. And though the answers didn't always come, he found solace in the act of praying itself, in the knowledge that he was not alone.

Slowly, the bitterness that had taken root in his heart began to fade, replaced by a cautious hope. He didn't know what the future held, didn't know if his marriage could be saved, or if he would find another job. But he was starting to believe that, whatever happened, he would be okay. He would survive, and maybe, just maybe, he would come out of this stronger than before. As the weeks turned into months, Alex found himself drawn back to the things that had once brought him joy. He began volunteering at the church, helping with the youth group, and participating in the men's Bible study. He reconnected with old friends, who welcomed him back with open arms, their support a balm to his wounded spirit. And slowly, he began to open up to Pastor John, sharing the pain and the doubts that had consumed him in those dark days. Pastor John listened without judgment, offering words of comfort and encouragement, reminding Alex that it was okay to struggle, to question, to doubt. Faith, he said, was not about having all the answers, but about trusting that God was with you, even in the uncertainty.

Bit by bit, Alex started to believe that again. He started to see the small miracles in everyday life—the kindness of a friend, the beauty of a sunset, the peace that came from a quiet moment of prayer. And though the road ahead was still uncertain, he knew that he was not walking it alone.

# CHAPTER 3

The weeks stretched into months, each one blending into the next as Alex's world remained stubbornly gray. His days were a relentless cycle of disappointment and desperation, each new setback adding weight to the burden he carried.

The job search had become a full-time job in itself. Mornings were spent scouring job boards and crafting carefully tailored resumes, while afternoons were spent at job fairs and interviews that often ended in rejection. The rejections piled up, each one a blow to Alex's already fragile self-esteem. He began to feel like a failure, the job loss and Lisa's betrayal merging into a singular, overwhelming sense of inadequacy.

At home, the atmosphere was thick with tension. Alex and Lisa spoke to each other in clipped, terse sentences, their conversations dominated by the practicalities of their situation rather than any real connection. Emma, their teenage daughter, seemed to retreat further into her own world, her laughter a rare sound in the house. The strained silence was punctuated only by the occasional argument over bills or the mounting stress. The financial strain was becoming unbearable. Bills that had once been manageable now felt like an avalanche, each due date a reminder of their dwindling savings. Alex and Lisa had been forced to dip into their emergency fund, a decision that filled them both with dread. The looming threat of foreclosure on their home was a constant, nagging worry that refused to go away.

One evening, as Alex sat at the kitchen table surrounded by unopened envelopes and overdue notices, he felt a wave of despair so profound it was almost physical. The walls of their home, once a haven, now felt like a cage. The papers before him were a stark reminder of their precarious situation, each one a symbol of failure.

Lisa walked in, her expression tired and drawn. "We need to talk," she said quietly, sitting down opposite Alex.

He looked up, his eyes hollow. "About what? We don't have much choice left."

Lisa's gaze fell to the table, her voice trembling. "I think we should talk to a financial advisor. Maybe they can help us find a way out of this mess."

Alex's heart sank. He knew she was right; they needed professional help. But the thought of facing their financial disaster head-on was almost too much to bear. And he still wasn't totally on okay terms with her after what happened.

"I know," he said, his voice heavy. "I just don't know if it's going to be enough."

Lisa reached out and touched his hand, a rare gesture of comfort. "We have to try," she said. "We can't give up."

Alex nodded, though he wasn't sure he believed it. The idea of fighting on, of trying to salvage what was left of their life, felt like an exercise in futility. He was exhausted, both physically and emotionally, and the prospect of dragging himself through one more appointment, one more failed attempt at finding a solution, was almost too overwhelming. That night, as Alex lay in bed, he found it difficult to sleep. The weight of his troubles pressed down on him, each worry and fear combining into a crushing heaviness. The darkness of the room seemed to reflect the darkness in his mind, an oppressive gloom that made it hard to breathe. He tried to pray, to find some semblance of comfort in the spiritual practice that had once been a source of solace. But the words felt hollow, the prayers empty. He questioned the very existence of God, the fairness of life, and whether there was any point in continuing to hold on to faith when it seemed like everything he had ever relied upon had crumbled. He was caught in a spiral of doubt and despair, a vortex that seemed impossible to escape. The emotional and financial strain was taking its toll, leaving him feeling isolated and abandoned.

Alex's isolation grew more profound as he continued to retreat from his social circle. He stopped answering calls from friends, avoided social gatherings, and became increasingly withdrawn. The only interactions he had were with Lisa and Emma, and even those were strained. The joy he had once found in relationships and social connections seemed to have evaporated, replaced by a profound sense of loneliness. He avoided the church, the very place that had once been a source of comfort. The thought of sitting through a service, of pretending to be okay when he was anything but, was more than he could bear. It was easier to stay home, to wallow in his despair, than to face the uncomfortable reality of his situation.

One Sunday morning, as the sun streamed through the window and the neighborhood began to stir, Alex found himself alone in the house. Lisa and Emma had gone to church, leaving him in the silence of their empty home. The solitude was both a comfort and a torment, a space where he could be alone with his thoughts and his pain. He wandered through the house aimlessly, his movements mechanical. He found himself in the living room, where a small stack of unopened mail lay on the coffee table. He picked up a letter, its envelope bearing the return address of a creditor. With a sigh, he tore it open and scanned the contents. The words were harsh, a reminder of the financial strain they were under. He tossed the letter aside, feeling a fresh wave of hopelessness. Sitting down on the couch, he glanced around the room. It was a space filled with memories—family photos, Emma's artwork, and the remnants of a life that felt increasingly distant. The weight of it all was almost too much to bear. In his despair, Alex picked up the Bible from the coffee table. It had been weeks since he last opened it, and the sight of it filled him with both hope and frustration. He flipped through the pages, looking for something, anything, that might offer him solace. But the words seemed to blur together, their meaning elusive.

He thought about the sermon he had heard months ago, before everything had begun to unravel. The message had been about trusting in God's plan, even when it was difficult to see the way forward. He had believed it then, had taken comfort in the idea that there was a purpose behind everything. But now, that faith seemed like a distant memory, a flickering candle in a storm. The hours passed slowly, each minute feeling like an eternity. Alex's mind was a whirlwind of despair and uncertainty, and he felt trapped in a cycle of negativity that he couldn't seem to break free from. The days blended together, each one marked by the same struggles and the same sense of hopelessness.

Despite the overwhelming darkness, there was a faint glimmer of hope that refused to be extinguished. It came in the form of a brief encounter at the grocery store. Alex was there, pushing a cart through the aisles, his mind preoccupied with the list of items he needed to buy and the mounting stress of his situation. As he turned a corner, he nearly collided with a woman who was browsing the cereal aisle. She looked up, startled, and Alex mumbled an apology. The woman smiled warmly, and for a moment, Alex was struck by the kindness in her eyes.

"Don't worry about it," she said. "We all have our days."

Alex nodded, unsure of how to respond. The brief interaction was a small thing, but it left a lingering impression. The woman's kindness, her genuine smile, was a small reminder that there was still goodness in the world, even if Alex felt like he was at the end of his rope. The encounter stayed with him as he continued his shopping. For the first time in a while, he found himself thinking that maybe, just maybe, there was still hope. It was a fleeting thought, but it was enough to spark a tiny ember of determination within him.

That night, as he lay in bed, Alex found himself thinking about the woman at the grocery store. Her kindness, her smile, had been a small beacon of light in the darkness. It wasn't a solution to his problems, but it was a reminder that there was still goodness, still hope, even in the midst of his struggles. He decided to take a small step, to try and re-engage with the world, even if it was just in a small way. The next day, he reached out to a former colleague, someone he hadn't spoken to in months. It felt awkward and uncomfortable, but it was a start. He made an appointment with a financial advisor, determined to face their financial challenges head-on. As he began to take these small steps, he felt a shift within himself. It wasn't a dramatic change, but it was a start. The hope that had seemed so elusive was beginning to take root, and Alex was starting to believe that, despite the darkness, there was still a path forward.

The journey ahead would be long and difficult, but for the first time in a while, Alex felt a sense of resolve. He was ready to face his challenges, to confront his fears, and to rebuild his life, one step at a time.

Determined to reconnect with his faith, Alex decided to visit another church. It was a modest building nestled in a quiet part of town, far from the grandiose architecture of his old church. He hoped that a change of scenery might rekindle his spiritual connection, offering a fresh perspective and, perhaps, some much-needed solace. On a crisp Sunday morning, Alex arrived early, taking a seat near the back of the sanctuary. The church was small but inviting, with simple wooden pews and stained-glass windows that cast colorful patterns on the floor. The congregation, a mix of young families and elderly couples, chatted quietly before the service began. As the service started, the pastor—a young man with an energetic presence—took the pulpit. His sermon was lively and engaging, filled with anecdotes and passionate declarations. But for Alex, the words seemed to bounce off him like rain off a slick surface. The sermon's upbeat tone felt out of sync with his inner turmoil. He struggled to connect with the message, feeling more disconnected from God than ever.

The music, though pleasant, did little to lift Alex's spirits. The hymns and contemporary worship songs blended into a background hum, failing to reach the places of pain and doubt within him. The smiles and greetings exchanged by the congregation seemed foreign, their warmth an uninvited reminder of his own isolation. After the service, Alex lingered near the exit, hoping to find some solace in conversation with others. He introduced himself to a few people, trying to engage in small talk, but the interactions were superficial and brief. He found himself yearning for the deep, meaningful connections he had once felt in his previous church, but those seemed elusive here. Feeling deflated, Alex walked out of the church and into the parking lot. The morning sun was bright, but it did little to brighten his mood. He got into his car and sat there for a few moments, staring at the dashboard. His heart was heavy, and the doubts he had tried to suppress came flooding back with renewed intensity. He questioned whether he was doing the right thing by trying to reconnect with his faith. Maybe he was expecting too much from a single visit, but the failure to find the comfort he had hoped for left him feeling even more adrift. The separation he felt from God seemed more pronounced, a chasm that no amount of effort could bridge.

Driving home, Alex wrestled with his emotions. The new church had not offered the reprieve he had sought; instead, it had highlighted his feelings of disconnection and disillusionment. He was on a journey to rediscover his faith, but today had been a setback, not the breakthrough he had hoped for. As he arrived home, the house was quiet. Lisa and Emma were still out, and Alex found himself alone with his thoughts. He sat down at the kitchen table, staring at the empty space where their meals used to be shared. The emptiness of the house mirrored the emptiness he felt inside.

Despite the discouragement, Alex knew he couldn't give up. He had to continue seeking, continue trying to reconnect, even if the process was slower and more painful than he had anticipated. He reached for the Bible on the table, its pages worn from use. He opened it to a random passage, hoping for some semblance of guidance or comfort.

The words on the page seemed to offer little solace, but Alex clung to the hope that this was just another step on his journey. He realized that faith, like any meaningful relationship, required patience and perseverance. It wasn't something that could be rekindled overnight, and it was okay to struggle along the way. As the day drew to a close, Alex resolved to keep moving forward. He would continue to explore, to seek, and to confront his doubts head-on. The path to reconnecting with his faith might be fraught with challenges, but he was determined to keep walking it, no matter how difficult it might be. The journey was far from over, and the road ahead was uncertain. But Alex knew that giving up was not an option. He had to hold on to hope, however faint, and trust that, eventually, he would find the way back to the faith that had once been a cornerstone of his life.

Alex arrived home feeling the weight of the morning's disappointment. The house was quiet, save for the faint sounds of Lisa and Emma chatting in the kitchen. As he entered, the smell of something hearty and comforting wafted through the air, a stark contrast to the emptiness he felt inside.

Lisa glanced up from the stove as he walked in, her face brightening with a mixture of relief and concern. "Hey, you're home early," she said, her voice warm and inviting. "I made your favorite—lasagna. I thought it might cheer you up."

Alex managed a weak smile, though it didn't reach his eyes. The promise of a comforting meal seemed incongruent with his mood. "Thanks, Lisa," he said quietly. "But I'm not really hungry right now."

Lisa's brow furrowed slightly, her concern evident. "Are you sure? It's just about ready. Maybe a little bit of food will help."

He shook his head, not trusting himself to speak without his voice betraying the depth of his sorrow. "No, I'm fine. I just... I need to be alone for a bit."

Lisa hesitated, then nodded, understanding but clearly worried. "Alright. If you change your mind, I'll be here."

Alex offered a brief nod before heading upstairs. Each step felt heavier than the last as he climbed the stairs, the weight of his despair dragging him down. He reached the bedroom, the familiar space feeling like a refuge yet a prison all at once.

The room was dimly lit by the soft afternoon light filtering through the curtains. He went to the bed and sat down, the sight of the rumpled sheets a stark reminder of how far his life had drifted from normalcy. He lay back, staring at the ceiling, feeling an overwhelming sense of emptiness and isolation.

The visit to the new church had been a failure, a bitter reminder of the distance he felt from his faith. The vibrant energy of the service had only highlighted his own emotional desolation. He closed his eyes, trying to escape the torrent of feelings swirling within him, but the effort was futile.

His thoughts turned inward, replaying the morning's events and his growing sense of disconnection. The tears began to fall, slowly at first, then with increasing intensity. He sobbed quietly, the sound muffled by the pillow beneath his head. Each sob was a release, a letting go of the pent-up anguish that had been building inside him for so long.

He cried until he was emotionally spent, his body trembling with the force of his sobs. The tears flowed unchecked, soaking into the pillow as his cries grew softer and softer. Exhausted by the emotional outpouring, Alex's sobs eventually subsided, leaving him drained and numb.

In the dim light of the room, Alex's breathing grew uneven, the tears having washed over him like a cleansing rain. He lay there, his face wet and his heart heavy, as sleep began to overtake him. The weight of the day's disappointment and his own sorrow lulled him into a deep, fitful sleep.

As he drifted off, the loneliness and heartache seemed to recede, if only for a moment. The darkness of sleep enveloped him, offering a temporary escape from the relentless pain of his waking life.

# CHAPTER 4

The house seemed quieter than usual, the ticking of the old wall clock echoing through the living room as Alex stared at the stack of unopened bills on the coffee table. Each envelope felt like a brick, building a wall that was slowly closing in around him. The foreclosure notice lay on top, its bold red lettering searing into his mind. He had always thought that rock bottom was a metaphor, but here it was, staring him in the face in the form of a legal notice. They were about to lose the house. The home where they'd raised Emma, where they'd celebrated birthdays, anniversaries, and where, until recently, life had felt safe and predictable.

Lisa was in the kitchen, her voice low as she talked on the phone. She hadn't said much since their last argument, but Alex knew she was still trying to hold everything together in her own way. They both were. But it wasn't enough. It hadn't been enough for a while now.

Alex stood, the simple act feeling heavy, as though the gravity in the room had doubled. He walked to the doorway and leaned against the frame, watching Lisa as she ended the call. She looked up at him, her eyes tired, a shadow of the woman he once knew.

"We can't keep doing this, Lisa," Alex said, his voice rough from days of silence.

She nodded, her hands trembling as she placed the phone on the counter. "I know, Alex. I've been looking at places near my parents. Maybe we should consider moving in with them, just for a little while. Until we can get back on our feet."

The thought of moving in with Lisa's parents felt like another blow to his pride, but what choice did they have? The clock was ticking, and they were running out of options. He wanted to argue, to refuse, but there was nothing left in him to fight with. The man who once provided for his family, who stood tall and proud, was now just a shell.

"I met someone today," Alex said, the words coming out before he could think them through. "At the food bank."

Lisa looked at him, a mixture of surprise and curiosity in her eyes. "Food bank?"

"Yeah… I didn't want to tell you. I just… I just needed to do something, anything, to feel useful."

"What did he say?" she asked, softening her tone.

"His name's Pastor John. We talked for a while. He said some things that… I don't know, made me think. He said suffering has a purpose, that it can lead to something better if you let it. Invited me to a support group at his church."

Lisa took a deep breath and stepped closer. "Do you think it'll help?"

"I don't know," Alex admitted. "But I need to try something. We need to try something."

Lisa nodded. "Maybe we both do."

For the first time in weeks, Alex felt a small spark of hope. It was faint, barely more than a flicker, but it was there. He wasn't sure what he would find at that church or if Pastor John's words would offer any real solace. But as he looked at Lisa, standing there with him in the quiet of their kitchen, he knew one thing: they couldn't keep going like this. Rock bottom was a place he never thought he'd find himself, but maybe, just maybe, it was also the place where they could start to rebuild.

The next morning, Alex stood in front of the small, modest church. He hesitated at the steps, feeling out of place, unsure if he belonged here or anywhere anymore. But something Pastor John said kept replaying in his mind: "Suffering is not the end, Alex; it's the beginning of a journey."

He pushed open the heavy door and stepped inside. The sanctuary was quiet, bathed in the soft glow of sunlight filtering through stained glass windows. The smell of polished wood and the faint scent of old candles greeted him, grounding him in a way he hadn't felt in months.

Pastor John was there, talking to a few people near the front. When he saw Alex, he excused himself and walked over, a warm smile on his face.

"I'm glad you came, Alex," he said, shaking his hand firmly. "It's a good first step."

"Feels like the only step I can take right now," Alex replied, his voice tinged with the exhaustion of the past months.

Pastor John nodded. "That's all you need to do. Just one step at a time."

Alex followed him into a small room off the side of the sanctuary where a few people had gathered. The room was filled with mismatched chairs, and a circle of people sat quietly, each one carrying their own burdens, their own stories of loss and struggle.

As the group began to share, Alex listened, the weight of his own problems feeling a little less isolating. He realized that he wasn't alone in his suffering, that others had faced their own versions of rock bottom. When it was his turn to speak, the words came slowly, haltingly at first, but then they flowed out of him like a river that had been dammed up for far too long.

"I lost my job," he began, his voice shaky. "And my home. My marriage… I don't know if it's going to survive this. I feel like I've lost everything."

Heads nodded around the circle, and Pastor John gave him an encouraging smile.

"But you're here," Pastor John said gently. "And that means something. It means you're willing to fight, even if you don't feel like you have the strength."

Alex felt a tear slip down his cheek, quickly wiping it away. "I don't know what to do."

"That's okay," someone in the group said. "None of us did when we started. But you'll figure it out. We all will. Together."

For the first time in a long while, Alex didn't feel completely lost. He was still at the bottom, but maybe, just maybe, he had found a foothold to start climbing back up.

Pastor John leaned forward, a thoughtful expression crossing his face as he studied Alex. "We have a group meeting tonight," he said, his tone gentle but inviting. "It's more than just a support group—it's a fellowship. We gather to share our experiences, not just the hard times, but the moments that changed us. It's a way to connect with others and to remind ourselves that even in the darkest moments, we're not alone."

Alex hesitated, the idea of sharing even more of himself with strangers feeling daunting. But there was something in Pastor John's eyes, a sincerity that made him feel safe, if only for a moment.

"I don't know if I'm ready for that," Alex admitted.

"No one ever is, at first," Pastor John replied with a reassuring smile. "But you might find that listening to others helps you understand your own journey better. And when you're ready, you can share your own story. There's no pressure."

Alex thought about it for a moment. The walls he had built around himself over the past few months had become suffocating, and while he wasn't sure he could tear them down completely, maybe he could lower them a little, just for tonight.

"Alright," Alex finally said. "I'll come."

Pastor John patted his shoulder. "You won't regret it."

That evening, Alex returned to the church, the parking lot half-full with cars. The sun had set, casting long shadows across the ground, but the lights from the church gave the place a warm, welcoming glow. Alex took a deep breath and walked inside, following the sounds of quiet conversation to a large room filled with people. The room was set up with round tables, each with a small centerpiece of candles and flowers. The atmosphere was relaxed, almost festive, with the smell of coffee and freshly baked bread in the air. People were mingling, some in deep conversation, others laughing softly as they shared stories. The noise level was low, respectful, but there was an underlying energy of connection, of community.

Pastor John spotted Alex from across the room and waved him over. "I'm glad you made it," he said, handing him a cup of coffee. "Why don't you sit with us? We're just about to get started."

Alex nodded, taking the coffee with a murmured thanks, and followed Pastor John to a table where a few others were already seated. He recognized one of the faces from the support group earlier, a middle-aged woman with kind eyes who smiled at him as he sat down.

"Good to see you again," she said. "I'm Sarah."

"Alex," he replied, offering a small smile in return.

"Everyone, let's gather around," Pastor John called out, his voice carrying easily across the room. The conversations slowly died down as people took their seats, the room settling into a comfortable quiet.

"Tonight," Pastor John began, "we're here to do what we do best—share. This group isn't about perfection; it's about progress. We all have stories, some painful, some joyful, but each one of them has shaped us into who we are today. And by sharing these stories, we help each other grow, heal, and find our way forward."

He looked around the room, his gaze gentle and encouraging. "Who would like to start?"

For a moment, there was silence, the kind that held a weight of anticipation. Then, a man across the table from Alex cleared his throat. He was older, with silver hair and a worn face that spoke of a life lived with both struggle and grace.

"I'll go," the man said, his voice steady. "My name's Tom. I've been coming to this group for about five years now. And when I first walked through those doors, I was a different man. Angry, lost… I'd just buried my wife of forty years, and I didn't know how to live without her."

Alex listened intently as Tom spoke, his voice filled with a deep, quiet pain. Tom described the years he spent in isolation, pushing people away, drowning in grief, until one day, a neighbor invited him to this very church. It was here, Tom explained, that he began to heal, slowly finding his way back to the world, to people, and to a new kind of life.

"It wasn't easy," Tom said, his eyes misting over. "But this group, these people… they brought me back. They reminded me that even though I'd lost so much, I wasn't alone. And that's what I want to pass on to you all tonight—none of us are alone."

The room was silent for a moment, the weight of Tom's story hanging in the air, before another person spoke up, sharing their own journey through addiction and recovery, then another about overcoming severe illness. Each story was different, but the common thread was resilience, the ability to keep going even when everything seemed lost. As the stories continued, Alex found himself getting drawn into the rhythm of the conversation, the ebb and flow of emotion, and the strength of the human spirit that each person displayed. For the first time in months, he felt something inside him shift. It wasn't a dramatic change, but a small, almost imperceptible crack in the armor he'd built around his heart. Toward the end of the evening, Pastor John turned to Alex.

"Would you like to share anything, Alex? There's no pressure, but we'd love to hear from you."

Alex hesitated, feeling the familiar knot of anxiety tightening in his chest. But as he looked around the room, at the faces filled with understanding and acceptance, he realized that this was exactly where he needed to be.

"I've been struggling," Alex began, his voice low and unsure. "I lost my job, and with it, I feel like I lost my sense of purpose. Everything just fell apart after that. My family, my faith… everything. I'm not sure how to move forward, or even if I can."

The room was quiet, everyone listening intently, giving Alex the space to express himself without judgment.

"But," Alex continued, his voice growing a little stronger, "hearing all of you tonight… it makes me think that maybe there's hope. Maybe I'm not as alone as I thought."

Pastor John smiled warmly. "You're not alone, Alex. And you don't have to go through this by yourself. We're all here to walk this journey with you, one step at a time."

As the meeting wound down and people began to leave, Alex stayed behind, lingering in the warmth of the room, the feeling of connection still buzzing in his chest. He exchanged a few words with Pastor John, who reassured him that the door was always open, and that he was welcome anytime.

When Alex finally stepped outside into the cool night air, he felt different—lighter, maybe even a little hopeful. The road ahead was still uncertain, but for the first time, he felt like he might actually have the strength to walk it, one step at a time.

# CHAPTER 5

The morning light filtered through the thin curtains in the small guest room where Alex had spent a restless night. Despite the tension at home, he had stayed awake thinking about the stories he had heard at the church. Those people, with their raw honesty and resilience, had sparked something in him. It wasn't quite hope, but maybe the beginnings of it—a small ember in the ashes of what his life had become. He glanced at the clock on the nightstand: 6:30 a.m. The house was quiet, the world outside just beginning to stir. He hadn't slept much, but for the first time in a while, he didn't feel as if the weight of the world was crushing him.

As he dressed, Alex replayed the conversation he'd had with Pastor John after the group meeting. The pastor had suggested that Alex come by again, and had mentioned that they were meeting for a casual breakfast at a local diner this morning. It wasn't a formal church event, just a few of the guys from the group getting together to talk, laugh, and share.

It was an invitation Alex would have usually declined. But today, he felt a pull, an urge to be around others, to hear more of those stories that had begun to soften the hard edges of his despair.

By the time Alex arrived at the diner, the sun was fully up, casting a golden hue across the modest building. Inside, the smell of coffee and frying bacon greeted him, along with the soft murmur of morning conversations. The diner was cozy, with worn booths and a counter lined with regulars sipping their coffee and reading the morning paper.

Alex spotted Pastor John in the back corner, laughing with two other men from the group. They waved him over as soon as he walked in, their smiles warm and welcoming.

"Alex!" Pastor John greeted him with a hearty handshake. "Glad you could make it."

"Good to see you again," said Tom, the older man who had shared his story of loss the night before. He was dressed casually, a stark contrast to the somber tone of his story, with a twinkle in his eye that suggested a man who had made peace with his past.

"Morning, Alex," said another man, Greg, who Alex recognized as one of the quieter members of the group. He was younger, maybe in his late thirties, with a serious expression that softened when he smiled.

"Hey," Alex replied, feeling a little out of place but grateful for the warmth of their welcome.

They slid into a booth, and a waitress appeared almost immediately, pouring Alex a cup of coffee without needing to ask. She was older, with a kind face and an easy manner, calling everyone "honey" as she took their orders.

The conversation was light at first, centered around everyday things—sports, the weather, work. But as the plates of pancakes and eggs arrived, the conversation naturally shifted, becoming deeper, more reflective.

"So, Alex," Pastor John began after a lull in the conversation, "how are you feeling after last night?"

Alex took a sip of his coffee, thinking. "Better, I think. It's been a long time since I felt connected to anything or anyone. Listening to everyone's stories... it made me realize I'm not the only one going through this."

"That's the beauty of it," Tom said, cutting into his pancakes. "When you're in the thick of it, you feel like you're the only one suffering. But we've all been there, in one way or another. And sometimes, just knowing that makes it easier to get through the day."

Greg nodded in agreement. "This group saved my life," he said quietly. "I was on the edge, ready to give up. But then I found this place, these people, and it gave me something to hold on to. It's still hard, but at least now I know I don't have to do it alone."

Alex looked at Greg, surprised by the vulnerability in his words. It was the first time he'd seen someone his own age express that kind of emotion so openly. It was both comforting and disconcerting.

"I'm trying to figure out what to do next," Alex admitted. "My life feels like it's been turned upside down. I don't even know where to start."

"Start small," Pastor John suggested. "One day at a time, one step at a time. You're not going to rebuild everything overnight. But with each step you take, you'll start to feel stronger, more in control."

Greg leaned forward, his expression serious. "That's what worked for me. I set small goals—just getting out of bed some days, or making a phone call I'd been avoiding. It wasn't much, but each time I did it, I felt a little better, a little more like I was taking back my life."

Alex nodded, the advice sinking in. Small steps. He could do that. He had to do that. "What about work?" he asked. "I feel like I need to do something, even if it's not what I used to do. Just to feel useful again."

"There's a grocery store not far from here that's looking for part-time help," Tom said. "It's not much, but it's a start. Might give you a chance to get out of the house, earn a little money, and clear your head."

It wasn't what Alex wanted to hear—after years in a corporate job, the idea of working at a grocery store felt like a step backward. But as Tom said, it was a start. And right now, he needed to start somewhere, anywhere.

"I'll think about it," Alex said, though the idea of it weighed heavily on him.

"That's all you can do," Pastor John said, offering a reassuring smile. "And remember, we're here for you, every step of the way."

Later that day, Alex found himself standing outside the grocery store, his breath fogging in the cool afternoon air. The store was busy, the parking lot filled with people going about their day, unaware of the quiet battle raging inside him. He hadn't planned on coming here, but after leaving the diner, he had driven around aimlessly, his thoughts circling back to what Pastor John and the others had said. Eventually, he had found himself in front of the store, wondering if he had the courage to walk inside and ask for a job.

It wasn't what he wanted, but it was what he needed.

Taking a deep breath, Alex pushed open the door and walked inside. The bright lights and the smell of produce and baked goods greeted him, and he approached the customer service desk, where a young woman with a friendly smile asked how she could help.

"I'm here about the job," Alex said, the words feeling foreign on his tongue.

"Great!" she replied, handing him an application form. "Just fill this out, and I'll get the manager for you."

As Alex sat at a small table in the corner, filling out the form, he thought about how far he had fallen, but also about how this might be the first step in climbing back up. It wasn't much, but it was something. And right now, something was better than nothing. By the time he finished, the manager—a middle-aged man with a kind face and a firm handshake—had arrived. They sat down together, and the conversation was straightforward. The job was basic, stocking shelves and helping customers, but it was steady work, and the manager seemed genuinely happy to have him.

"I know it might not be what you're used to," the manager said, "but we're a good team here. We take care of each other."

Alex nodded, feeling a small, surprising sense of relief. "That sounds good to me."

The next few days passed in a blur of early mornings and simple tasks. The work was hard and humbling, but it kept his mind occupied, and each day he came home feeling a little less lost. He still had a long way to go, but the routine gave him a sense of purpose, however small. He also started attending the support group more regularly, finding comfort in the familiarity of the faces and the shared experiences. Each session made him feel a little stronger, a little more ready to face the challenges ahead. And slowly, almost imperceptibly, Alex began to change. He found himself praying more, not with the desperation he had felt before, but with a quiet hope that maybe, just maybe, things would get better.

One evening, after another long day at work, Alex sat in his car outside the house, the engine idling as he stared at the front door. Inside, Lisa was waiting, and the tension between them had started to ease, if only slightly. They had begun talking more, sharing small moments of connection that hadn't been there before. As he turned off the engine and stepped out of the car, Alex realized that he was beginning to feel something he hadn't felt in a long time—gratitude. Not for the suffering, but for the small moments of grace that had begun to punctuate his days. He wasn't where he wanted to be, but for the first time, he felt like he was on the right path. When he walked through the door, Lisa was in the kitchen, preparing dinner. She looked up and smiled at him, a real smile that reached her eyes.

"How was your day?" she asked.

"Good," Alex replied, and for the first time in a long while, he meant it.

They sat down to dinner together, and as they ate, Alex couldn't help but think that maybe, just maybe, they were starting to find their way back to each other. It was a long road ahead, but with each small step, he was beginning to believe that they might actually make it.

The day had been long, and Alex was beginning to feel the strain of the constant activity. Stocking shelves, answering questions, and navigating the small challenges of his new job was exhausting but oddly satisfying. He was beginning to settle into a routine, finding a rhythm in the simple tasks that kept him grounded. Late in the afternoon, just as Alex was restocking the condiments aisle, he noticed an elderly woman shuffling slowly into the store. She was petite, her frame slightly hunched with age, and she moved with the careful, deliberate steps of someone who had learned to be cautious in a world that could often be overwhelming.

Alex watched her for a moment, noticing how she hesitated at the entrance, her eyes scanning the store as if trying to remember where everything was. Something about her reminded him of his own grandmother, who had passed away a few years back. She had the same air of quiet dignity, of someone who had seen much in life and yet still carried a softness in her heart.

He put down the box of jars he was arranging and approached her with a warm smile. "Good afternoon, ma'am. Can I help you find anything today?"

The elderly woman looked up at him, her eyes bright but a little tired. "Oh, thank you, young man," she said, her voice soft and wavering. "I'm looking for some condiments—ketchup, mustard, that sort of thing. And some fruit, too, if it's not too much trouble."

"Not trouble at all," Alex replied. "I'd be happy to help. Let's start with the condiments—they're just down this aisle."

He led her slowly down the aisle, making sure to keep his pace slow enough for her to follow comfortably. She moved with care, occasionally stopping to examine a product or to rest her hand on the cart for support.

"What kind of ketchup are you looking for?" Alex asked as they reached the section filled with rows of bottles.

"Oh, just the regular kind," she said, squinting at the labels. "But it has to be low sodium—my doctor's orders."

Alex quickly found a low-sodium ketchup and placed it in her cart. "There you go. Is there anything else you need from this aisle?"

She glanced around, her brow furrowed in concentration. "Maybe some mayonnaise, and… oh, some pickles. My granddaughter loves pickles."

As they gathered the items, Alex couldn't help but notice how frail she seemed, how each movement seemed to cost her more energy than it should. But despite that, there was a gentleness to her, a quiet determination that reminded him of the stories he had heard at the support group. When they had finished with the condiments, Alex guided her to the produce section, where she carefully examined the fruits, picking up apples and oranges with a practiced hand. She seemed to take her time, inspecting each piece of fruit with a care that spoke of years of experience.

"These apples look lovely," she said, placing a few in her cart. "But I think I'll need some help reaching those bananas up there."

Alex reached for the bananas she pointed out and handed them to her. She smiled, a genuine warmth in her eyes. "Thank you, dear. You're very kind."

"It's no problem at all," Alex said, feeling a small surge of satisfaction. He wasn't doing anything extraordinary, just helping her shop, but it felt good to be useful, to make someone else's day a little easier.

For the next hour, Alex stayed by her side as she slowly made her way through the store, picking out a few more items and chatting softly about her family, her late husband, and her weekly trips to the grocery store, which she looked forward to as a small adventure in her otherwise quiet life.

"My granddaughter usually comes with me," she said at one point, her voice tinged with a hint of sadness. "But she's been so busy with work lately. I didn't want to bother her, so I thought I'd manage on my own today."

Alex nodded, listening to her story as they walked. "It's great that you're still getting out and about," he said. "But if you ever need a hand with anything, you can always ask. We're happy to help."

She smiled up at him, her eyes soft with gratitude. "You're a good man, young man. Thank you for being so patient with me today."

By the time they reached the checkout, the store was beginning to quiet down, the evening rush starting to taper off. Alex helped her unload her cart onto the conveyor belt, making sure everything was carefully placed and bagged. As the cashier rang up her items, the elderly woman turned to Alex once more.

"You've been such a blessing today," she said, her voice filled with genuine emotion. "It's not often I come across someone as kind as you. You've made my day so much easier, and I can't thank you enough for that."

Alex felt a lump form in his throat, a wave of unexpected emotion washing over him. He hadn't done anything remarkable, but the sincerity in her words touched something deep inside him, something that had been starved for this kind of connection, this kind of purpose.

"I'm just glad I could help," he said, his voice a little rough.

She reached out and gently squeezed his hand. "You did more than help, dear. You made me feel cared for. That's a rare gift these days."

Alex helped her out to her car, loading the groceries into the trunk with the same care she had taken in selecting them. As she got into the driver's seat, she waved one last time, her smile bright and genuine.

"Take care of yourself, young man. And remember, kindness comes back to you in ways you might not expect."

"I'll remember that," Alex replied, watching as she slowly drove away.

As he walked back into the store, the heaviness that had followed him for so long seemed a little lighter. The encounter had been simple, ordinary even, but it had left him feeling fulfilled in a way he hadn't felt in months. It was as if, in those few hours, he had found a small piece of himself again, the part that cared deeply for others, that found joy in small acts of service. When he finally clocked out and headed home, there was a quiet satisfaction in his heart, a sense that maybe, just maybe, he was on the right path. He didn't have all the answers, and the road ahead was still uncertain, but for the first time in a long time, he felt like he was doing something that mattered.

As he stepped through the front door, the house was quiet. Lisa was reading in the living room, the soft glow of a lamp illuminating her face. She looked up as he entered, a small smile on her lips.

"How was work?" she asked.

Alex paused for a moment, thinking about the day, about the elderly woman and the unexpected fulfillment he had found in helping her.

"It was good," he said, his voice filled with a quiet confidence that surprised even him. "It was really good."

Lisa's smile widened, and for the first time in months, Alex felt a sense of peace settle over him as he sat down beside her. The road ahead was still long, but for tonight, he was content to just be, to rest in the simple satisfaction of a day well spent.

The days following his encounter with the elderly woman brought a subtle but significant shift in Alex's routine. Each morning, he found himself rising a little earlier, driven by a need that went beyond the responsibilities of his part-time job. There was something awakening within him, a desire to reconnect with a part of his life that he had neglected for too long. One evening, after a particularly quiet day at the store, Alex returned home feeling restless. The usual distractions—television, mindless scrolling through his phone—no longer held any appeal. Instead, he found himself standing in front of the bookshelf in the living room, his gaze lingering on a worn, leather-bound Bible that had once been a constant companion. He reached for it hesitantly, the weight of it familiar yet strange in his hands. It had been months, maybe even years, since he had last opened it with any real intention. Life had a way of crowding out the spiritual, leaving him too tired, too preoccupied to seek solace in its pages. But tonight was different. Tonight, he felt a pull, a quiet urging to find something more than the daily grind, something that could anchor him in the storm of uncertainty that had become his life.

He sat down on the couch, the house unusually still. Lisa had gone to bed early, and Emma was out with friends. For the first time in what felt like forever, Alex was alone with his thoughts—and with his faith. He opened the Bible, the pages crackling softly as they parted. He wasn't sure where to begin, so he let the book fall open on its own, trusting that it would lead him to where he needed to be. His eyes settled on a passage in the book of Psalms, one he had read many times before but that now seemed to speak directly to his weary soul:

"The Lord is my shepherd; I shall not want. He maketh me to lie down in green pastures: he leadeth me beside the still waters. He restoreth my soul: he leadeth me in the paths of righteousness for his name's sake." — Psalm 23:1-3

The words washed over him, soothing the raw edges of his spirit. He read them again, slower this time, letting their meaning sink in. *He restoreth my soul.* The phrase resonated deeply, as if it held a promise he had forgotten but desperately needed to remember. He closed his eyes, the Bible resting on his lap, and let out a long breath. The room around him seemed to fade away, leaving only the silence and the steady rhythm of his breathing. In that stillness, Alex began to pray—not with the polished, rehearsed prayers of his youth, but with raw, unfiltered honesty.

"God," he whispered, his voice trembling slightly, "I don't know where I'm going or how I'm going to get there. I've made mistakes, lost my way… but I want to come back. I need your help. I need… something more than what I've been holding on to."

The words came slowly at first, but as he spoke, they began to flow more freely, carrying with them the weight of all he had been carrying alone. He prayed for guidance, for strength, for forgiveness—for himself and for Lisa. He prayed for the wisdom to rebuild his life, to find a new purpose, and to mend the fractured relationships that had once been his anchor.

And as he prayed, a sense of peace began to settle over him, a quiet reassurance that, despite the uncertainty, he was not alone in this journey. It wasn't a dramatic revelation or a miraculous solution to his problems, but it was enough—a whisper of hope that perhaps, with faith and perseverance, he could find his way back to the life he was meant to live. When he finally opened his eyes, the room seemed brighter somehow, as if the act of prayer had lifted a veil from his heart. The burden he had been carrying for so long felt a little lighter, and for the first time in months, he felt the stirrings of hope take root in his soul.

Over the next few days, Alex made it a habit to carve out time for prayer and reflection, even if it was just a few minutes before bed or in the quiet moments before the store opened. He found himself turning more often to the Bible, seeking out passages that spoke to his current struggles, and finding comfort in the words that had guided countless others before him. The Bible became more than just a book; it became a lifeline, a source of wisdom and strength that he could draw upon when the weight of the world felt too heavy. As he delved deeper into its teachings, he began to see his challenges in a new light—not as insurmountable obstacles, but as opportunities for growth, for learning, for strengthening his faith.

One evening, after a particularly moving prayer session, Alex found himself reflecting on Pastor John's words about suffering and faith. He had been skeptical at first, resistant to the idea that there could be purpose in his pain. But now, with each passing day, he was beginning to understand. Suffering, he realized, had a way of stripping away the superficial, of forcing him to confront the core of who he was and what he believed. It had humbled him, brought him to his knees—literally and figuratively—and in that humility, he had found the beginnings of a deeper connection with God. As he closed the Bible that night, Alex felt a quiet determination take hold. He didn't have all the answers, and he knew there would be more struggles ahead, but he was no longer adrift. His faith, once a flickering candle, was now a steady flame, guiding him through the darkness.

And with that faith came a renewed sense of purpose, a belief that, no matter how uncertain the future might be, he had the strength to face it. Not alone, but with God's guidance, with the love of his family, and with the quiet but powerful conviction that he was on a path of healing and growth. As he drifted off to sleep that night, Alex felt a sense of peace settle over him, the kind that comes from knowing that, even in the midst of chaos, there is a greater plan at work—a plan that he was finally beginning to trust. And with that trust, he knew, would come the courage to rebuild, to forgive, and to find the joy that had eluded him for so long.

# CHAPTER 6

The morning sun streamed through the kitchen window as Alex sat at the table, his hands wrapped around a steaming cup of coffee. The warmth from the mug seeped into his palms, but his thoughts were elsewhere, swirling around the difficult conversation that lay ahead. The night before, he and Lisa had agreed that it was time to take the next step in mending their relationship—couples therapy. The idea of therapy had been hanging over them for weeks, ever since that tense argument where Lisa had first suggested it. At the time, Alex had been resistant, defensive even. The thought of exposing their deepest wounds to a stranger felt too raw, too vulnerable. But now, after the spiritual renewal he had begun to experience, he saw it differently. If they were going to rebuild what had been broken, they needed help, and he was ready to face that challenge, no matter how uncomfortable it might be.

Lisa entered the kitchen quietly, her hair still damp from the shower, and took a seat across from him. She looked at him with a mixture of apprehension and hope. The silence between them was heavy, charged with unspoken fears and lingering doubts.

"Are you ready for this?" Lisa asked, her voice soft but steady.

Alex nodded, his grip tightening around the mug. "I am. It's not going to be easy, but I think… I think we need it."

She reached across the table, her fingers brushing against his. The simple gesture carried a weight of its own, a tentative step toward the intimacy they had once taken for granted.

"We've both made mistakes," Lisa said, her eyes meeting his with an openness that hadn't been there in a long time. "But I want to try, Alex. I want us to heal."

"Me too," he replied, feeling the words settle into place like a promise.

Later that afternoon, they found themselves sitting in a small, warmly lit office. The room was cozy, with soft, inviting chairs and a large window that let in natural light. The walls were adorned with calming artwork—abstract pieces that seemed to evoke emotions without being overwhelming. Their therapist, Dr. Rachel Simmons, was a woman in her mid-forties with kind eyes and a calm demeanor. She had greeted them with a smile that was neither too cheerful nor too solemn, striking the right balance for what was sure to be a difficult conversation.

"Welcome," Dr. Simmons began as they settled into their seats. "I'm glad you both decided to come today. Therapy can be a challenging process, but it can also be incredibly rewarding if we're honest with each other."

Lisa nodded, and Alex took a deep breath, feeling the tension in the room build.

"I want you both to feel safe here," Dr. Simmons continued. "This is a place where you can express your thoughts and feelings without fear of judgment. We're here to explore what's been happening in your relationship and to find ways to rebuild the trust and connection that might have been lost."

The first session was difficult, as Alex had expected. They began by discussing the layoff and the impact it had on their lives. Alex talked about the fear and shame he had felt, the way it had eaten away at his confidence and made him withdraw from Lisa and Emma. Lisa, in turn, shared how she had felt overwhelmed by the changes, how she had turned to her work as a way to cope with the mounting stress, and eventually sought solace in the affair. When the conversation shifted to the affair, the atmosphere in the room grew heavy with emotion. Lisa spoke of her regret, of how she had been searching for something—comfort, validation, an escape— that she hadn't been able to find in their strained marriage. Alex listened, his heart aching with a mix of anger and sorrow, but he forced himself to stay open, to really hear her out.

"I know I hurt you," Lisa said, her voice trembling. "I hurt us. And I hate myself for that. But I want to make things right, Alex. I want to be better, for you and for Emma."

Alex swallowed hard, his emotions a tangled mess. He still felt the sting of betrayal, but he also saw the pain in Lisa's eyes, the genuine remorse that softened her words. He knew that forgiveness wasn't something that could happen overnight, but sitting there, in that room, he realized that he wanted to try.

"I want that too," he finally said, his voice thick with emotion. "I'm not sure how we'll get there, but I guess that I'm willing to try. I'm willing to put in the work."

The session ended with them setting goals for the future—small steps they could take to begin rebuilding their relationship. Dr. Simmons emphasized the importance of communication and honesty, encouraging them to check in with each other regularly, to be open about their needs and fears.

As they left the office, walking to the car in silence, Alex felt a strange mix of exhaustion and hope. The session had drained him emotionally, but it had also given him a sense of direction. They had taken the first step, and that was something.

Over the next few weeks, therapy became a regular part of their lives. The sessions were often intense, filled with tears, confessions, and difficult truths. But they were also healing. Each time they left Dr. Simmons's office, Alex and Lisa felt a little closer, a little more connected. They began to understand each other in new ways, recognizing the patterns that had led them astray and finding new ways to communicate. Outside of therapy, Alex's spiritual journey continued to deepen. He found himself drawn more and more to the Bible, to the wisdom and comfort it offered. Each morning, he began his day with a quiet moment of prayer and reflection, grounding himself in the faith that had once been such an integral part of his life. The verses he read spoke to him in ways they never had before. He found solace in passages about forgiveness and renewal, strength in the stories of those who had faced great trials and emerged stronger. He started keeping a journal, jotting down his thoughts and prayers, recording the small victories and the setbacks alike.

One evening, after a particularly intense therapy session, Alex felt the need to delve deeper into his Bible. He opened it to the book of Ephesians, drawn to the passages about love and marriage:

"Be completely humble and gentle; be patient, bearing with one another in love. Make every effort to keep the unity of the Spirit through the bond of peace." — Ephesians 4:2-3

The words resonated deeply with him. Humility, patience, love—these were the virtues he needed to cultivate, not just in his relationship with Lisa but within himself. He prayed for the strength to embody these qualities, to approach each day with a heart open to healing and growth. The next morning, as they sat down for breakfast, Alex felt a shift in the air between him and Lisa. It was subtle, but it was there—a sense of calm, of mutual respect that hadn't been present in months.

"Thank you for being willing to go to therapy," Lisa said softly as she poured them both a cup of coffee. "I know it's not easy."

Alex smiled, reaching across the table to take her hand. "Thank you too. For sticking with it, for wanting to make things better."

Lisa squeezed his hand, her eyes warm with gratitude. "I think we're getting there, Alex. Slowly, but we're getting there."

As the days turned into weeks, they continued to make progress—both in therapy and at home. They started spending more time together, not just as a couple but as a family. They took walks in the park, shared meals at the dinner table, and even began planning small weekend trips, rekindling the bond that had once been the foundation of their relationship. And through it all, Alex's faith remained his anchor. The more he prayed, the more he read, the stronger he felt—not just in his relationship with Lisa but in his sense of self. The spiritual growth he experienced was gradual, like the slow unfurling of a flower in bloom, but it was steady, and it brought with it a deepening sense of peace.

One Sunday, after a particularly uplifting church service, Alex sat on the porch with his Bible in hand, watching the sunset. The sky was awash with color—fiery oranges, deep purples, and soft pinks blending together in a breathtaking display of nature's beauty. As he watched the day fade into night, he felt a profound sense of gratitude. Gratitude for the chance to rebuild his life, for the love he and Lisa were slowly rediscovering, and for the faith that had guided him through the darkest times.

He opened his Bible to one of his favorite passages from the book of Romans:

"And we know that in all things God works for the good of those who love him, who have been called according to his purpose." — Romans 8:28

As he read the words, a smile spread across his face. He didn't know what the future held, but he knew that, whatever came, he would face it with faith, with love, and with the quiet strength that came from knowing he was not alone on this journey. And in that moment, as the last rays of sunlight dipped below the horizon, Alex felt a sense of peace that he hadn't felt in years—a peace that came from the knowledge that, with God's guidance and Lisa by his side, he was finally on the path to healing and redemption.

After weeks of making progress in therapy, Alex and Lisa found themselves facing another critical aspect of their recovery: their finances. The weight of their financial troubles had been a constant source of stress, a shadow that lingered over every decision they made. With the looming threat of foreclosure and the dwindling savings, they knew they couldn't afford to ignore it any longer.

One evening, after a particularly productive therapy session, Lisa brought up the idea as they sat down for dinner.

"I've been thinking," she began, her tone cautious yet resolute, "we've made some great strides in therapy, but there's another area we really need to address—our finances."

Alex looked up from his plate, a knot forming in his stomach. The mention of money had always been a sore spot, especially in recent months.

"I know," he admitted, his voice tinged with resignation. "But where do we even start? We're so far behind…"

Lisa reached across the table and took his hand, her grip firm and reassuring. "I've actually been researching financial advisors. I think it's time we get some professional help. We can't do this alone, Alex. We need someone who can help us create a plan, someone who can guide us through this mess." Alex hesitated, the idea of exposing their financial situation to a stranger making him uncomfortable. But he also knew that they couldn't keep avoiding it. If they were going to rebuild their lives, they needed to confront this head-on.

"Okay," he finally said, squeezing her hand. "Let's do it. Let's meet with a financial advisor."

Lisa smiled, relief washing over her features. "I actually found someone who comes highly recommended. Her name is Emily Grant. She specializes in helping families in financial crisis. I thought we could set up a meeting with her this week."

"Emily Grant," Alex repeated, the name feeling unfamiliar yet somehow comforting. "Sounds like a good place to start."

A few days later, they found themselves sitting in Emily's office, a modern space with clean lines and a calming palette of soft grays and blues. The atmosphere was professional yet welcoming, designed to put clients at ease as they faced some of life's most difficult challenges. Emily herself was a woman in her early forties, with a confident yet compassionate demeanor. She greeted them warmly, her handshake firm and her smile genuine.

"It's great to meet you both," she said as they took their seats across from her desk. "I understand that you're facing some significant financial challenges right now, and I want you to know that you're not alone. My job is to help you navigate this situation, to create a plan that works for your family, and to guide you toward a more stable financial future."

Alex nodded, feeling a mixture of anxiety and hope. "We're definitely in a tough spot," he admitted. "We've been struggling ever since I lost my job, and it feels like we're drowning in bills."

Emily listened attentively, her expression thoughtful as she absorbed their story. "I hear you, and I know how overwhelming it can be to face financial difficulties on top of everything else you're dealing with. The first thing I want to say is that there's always a way forward, even when it feels like there isn't."

She leaned forward slightly, her tone encouraging. "Before we dive into the specifics, I'd like to get a better understanding of your financial situation—your income, expenses, debts, and any assets you might have. This will help us create a clear picture of where you stand and what options are available to you."

Lisa pulled out a folder from her bag and handed it to Emily. "We've brought all our financial documents—bank statements, bills, everything. We thought it would be helpful."

"Perfect," Emily said, accepting the folder with a nod. "Let's go through these together, and then we'll discuss some potential strategies."

As they went through the documents, Emily asked a series of pointed questions, her approach thorough but nonjudgmental. She wanted to understand not just the numbers, but also the emotional context behind them—the choices that had led them here, the fears and hopes they had for the future. Alex found himself opening up more than he expected. There was something about Emily's calm, measured demeanor that made it easier to talk about the mistakes they had made, the moments of panic and despair that had driven some of their decisions.

After nearly an hour of discussion, Emily leaned back in her chair, her hands resting on the stack of papers before her. "Thank you for sharing all of this with me," she said, her voice warm. "I know it's not easy to lay everything out like this, but it's a crucial step in taking control of your finances."

She paused for a moment, organizing her thoughts. "Here's what I'm seeing: You're in a tough spot, but it's not hopeless. The good news is that you still have options. The first thing we need to do is create a realistic budget that reflects your current situation. This means cutting back on non-essential expenses and focusing on the basics—housing, food, utilities, and debt repayment."

Lisa nodded, absorbing the information. "We've already started cutting back, but it feels like we're still barely making a dent."

Emily smiled reassuringly. "That's normal, especially when you're dealing with significant debt. But with a structured plan, we can start to make progress. We'll also look into ways to increase your income—whether that's through Alex's part-time job, Lisa's work, or other opportunities you might not have considered yet."

Alex frowned slightly, the thought of finding more work weighing on him. "I've been trying to find a full-time job, but it's been tough. The job market is brutal right now."

"I understand," Emily said empathetically. "It's a challenging environment, but we'll explore all avenues. In the meantime, your part-time job is a start, and every little bit helps."

She glanced at Lisa. "We'll also need to address the looming foreclosure. It's crucial that we communicate with your mortgage lender as soon as possible. Sometimes lenders are willing to work with you if they know you're making an effort to get back on track. There might be options for loan modification or temporary forbearance, which could give you some breathing room."

Lisa looked at Alex, a flicker of hope in her eyes. "That could make a big difference."

Emily nodded. "It could. The key is to be proactive, to reach out before things escalate further. We'll draft a letter together and explore all available options. And remember, you're not doing this alone. I'm here to support you every step of the way."

As the meeting wrapped up, Emily handed them a detailed action plan. It was a roadmap of sorts, outlining the steps they needed to take in the coming weeks—from setting up a budget to contacting their mortgage lender and exploring additional income streams.

Alex looked at the plan, feeling a mix of emotions—relief that they had a path forward, but also the weight of the work that lay ahead. "Thank you," he said, his voice sincere. "This means a lot to us."

"You're welcome," Emily replied, her tone encouraging. "It's going to take time and effort, but I believe you can do this. You've already taken the hardest step by coming here and facing your situation head-on."

As they left Emily's office and walked to the car, Alex felt a strange sense of empowerment. The meeting had been intense, and the road ahead was daunting, but for the first time in a long while, he felt like they had a plan—a real, actionable plan that could lead them out of the financial mess they were in.

Lisa squeezed his hand as they got into the car, a small smile playing on her lips. "I feel like we can really do this, Alex. It's going to be hard, but we have a plan now. We're not just treading water anymore."

Alex nodded, feeling a sense of solidarity between them. "Yeah, we're moving forward. One step at a time."

That night, after Emma had gone to bed, Alex and Lisa sat down together to review the action plan. They made a list of priorities, dividing tasks between them and setting deadlines for each step. As they worked, the tension that had once plagued their discussions about money seemed to dissipate, replaced by a shared determination to rebuild their lives.

When they finally finished, Alex closed his notebook and looked at Lisa, feeling a deep sense of gratitude. "We're going to get through this," he said, his voice firm. "We're going to come out stronger on the other side."

Lisa smiled, her eyes reflecting the same hope. "We are," she agreed. "Together."

As they prepared for bed, Alex took a moment to reflect on how far they had come. They were still facing many challenges, but they were facing them together—with a renewed sense of trust, a plan for their future, and the strength of their faith to guide them.

Before turning in for the night, Alex knelt by the bed and said a quiet prayer, thanking God for the progress they had made and asking for continued guidance and strength. He felt a deep sense of peace as he climbed into bed, knowing that, step by step, they were on the path to healing—not just their finances, but their marriage and their lives. And with that, he drifted off to sleep.

In the weeks following their meeting with Emily, Alex and Lisa made a conscious effort to reconnect, not just financially but emotionally. The tension that had once characterized their interactions began to ease, replaced by a growing sense of partnership. They both understood that their journey to rebuild their marriage would be long and challenging, but they were committed to taking it one step at a time. One of the first changes they made was reinstating family dinners, something that had fallen by the wayside amidst the chaos of their lives. Emma, initially skeptical of this new routine, quickly warmed to the idea when she saw how her parents were trying to make an effort.

One evening, they gathered around the dinner table, the aroma of a home-cooked meal filling the kitchen. Alex had decided to take on cooking duties, trying out new recipes he found online. Tonight, it was a simple pasta dish with a fresh salad on the side. As they ate, the conversation flowed naturally. Emma talked about her day at school, recounting stories about her friends and upcoming projects. Alex and Lisa listened attentively, asking questions and laughing at her anecdotes. It was a far cry from the strained silences and clipped conversations that had characterized their meals in the recent past.

"So, how did your math test go?" Lisa asked, passing Emma the salad bowl.

Emma shrugged, a playful grin on her face. "Not bad. I think I aced it, actually."

Alex chuckled, feeling a surge of pride. "That's my girl! You're gonna make us proud yet."

Emma rolled her eyes, but the smile on her face showed that she appreciated the praise. "You guys are so cheesy," she said, but her tone was light, teasing.

After dinner, with the dishes cleared away, Alex and Lisa exchanged a glance. It was one of those moments where words weren't necessary—they both felt the warmth of a family evening well-spent.

"Want to go for a walk?" Lisa suggested as they finished up the kitchen chores. It had been a while since they had done something as simple as walking together, and the idea held an appeal that felt both nostalgic and new.

"Yeah," Alex agreed, drying his hands. "It's a nice night for it."

They told Emma they'd be back soon and stepped outside into the cool evening air. The sun had just set, casting the sky in shades of pink and orange. Their neighborhood, once bustling with the sounds of day, had settled into a peaceful quiet.

They started walking down the familiar streets, the rhythm of their steps in sync. The silence between them was comfortable, filled with the chirping of crickets and the rustle of leaves in the breeze. For the first few minutes, they simply enjoyed the tranquility, neither feeling the need to speak.

As they rounded a corner, Alex reached for Lisa's hand, threading his fingers through hers. It was a small gesture, but it felt significant—an acknowledgment of the bond they were slowly rebuilding.

"I missed this," Lisa said softly, glancing at him. "Just being together like this, without the weight of everything pressing down on us."

"Me too," Alex admitted. "It feels like we're finding our way back to each other."

They continued walking, eventually finding themselves at the park where they had spent countless hours during the early days of their relationship. The memories of those carefree times, when they had nothing but each other and endless possibilities, brought a smile to Alex's face.

"Remember this place?" Lisa asked, as they approached their favorite bench, nestled under an old oak tree. It was the spot where they had first talked about their dreams for the future, where they had planned their lives together.

"How could I forget?" Alex replied, squeezing her hand. "This was where we used to dream about what our lives would be like… before all the craziness."

They sat down on the bench, the wood smooth and worn from years of use. The park was almost empty, the only sounds the distant hum of traffic and the occasional chirp of a bird settling in for the night.

"We've been through a lot," Lisa said after a moment, her voice thoughtful. "More than I ever imagined we would. But sitting here with you, I realize that despite everything, I still believe in those dreams we talked about."

Alex looked at her, seeing the sincerity in her eyes. "So do I," he said, his voice firm. "We've been knocked down, but we're still standing. And as long as we're together, I believe we can still build the life we always wanted."

They sat in silence for a while longer, lost in their thoughts, the comfort of each other's presence enough. When they finally stood to leave, the park was enveloped in darkness, the streetlights casting long shadows on the path.

In the days that followed, Alex and Lisa continued to find small ways to reconnect. They made time for walks, exploring their old haunts and discovering new ones. They shared morning coffees on the porch, enjoying the quiet moments before the day began. Sometimes they'd go out for ice cream, just like they used to when they first started dating. These simple, everyday moments became the foundation of their renewed relationship. Each shared laugh, each conversation about the future, each gentle touch was a brick in the wall they were rebuilding—stronger, more resilient than before. One weekend, they decided to visit the beach, a place that had always held a special place in their hearts. It was where they had gone on their first trip together, where they had taken Emma as a baby, her tiny feet sinking into the sand for the first time. As they walked along the shore, the waves lapping at their feet, they talked about their dreams once more—dreams that had changed, matured, but were no less cherished.

"Maybe someday, when things are more stable, we could think about buying a little place by the water," Lisa mused, her eyes on the horizon. "It doesn't have to be anything big or fancy. Just a place where we can escape, recharge… a place that's ours."

Alex smiled, imagining it. "I like that idea. A place where we can relax and enjoy the simple things… where we can grow old together."

Lisa leaned into him, resting her head on his shoulder as they walked. "It's not the big things that matter most, is it?" she said quietly. "It's moments like this."

"No," Alex agreed, feeling the truth of her words deep in his bones. "It's the little things, the everyday moments that make a life."

They spent the rest of the day at the beach, savoring each moment—the warmth of the sun, the feel of the sand between their toes, the sound of Emma's laughter as she splashed in the waves. It was a perfect day, not because everything was perfect, but because they were together, healing, and finding joy in the simple pleasures of life. As the sun began to set, casting the sky in hues of orange and pink, they sat on the sand, watching the day fade into night. Alex wrapped his arm around Lisa, pulling her close, content in the knowledge that they were on the right path—one step at a time, one small moment at a time. And as they drove home that evening, with Emma dozing in the back seat and the radio playing softly, Alex felt a deep sense of peace. They were not just rebuilding their marriage, but their family, their life—brick by brick, moment by moment. And he knew, with unwavering certainty, that they would make it through, stronger and more united than ever before.

After weeks of working on their relationship, Alex and Lisa felt ready to take the next step in their financial recovery. The meeting with Emily, their new financial advisor, had already opened their eyes to the importance of careful planning and disciplined budgeting. Now, it was time to dive deeper into the numbers and make decisions that would ensure their future stability. They scheduled a follow-up meeting with Emily at her office, a bright and welcoming space that immediately put them at ease. As they sat across from her at a sleek wooden desk, Emily greeted them with a warm smile.

"I'm glad to see you both again," she began, spreading out a series of documents in front of them. "I've reviewed your financial situation in more detail since our last meeting, and I have some suggestions on how we can approach budgeting and debt management."

Alex and Lisa exchanged a glance, both feeling a mixture of anxiety and relief. They knew they had to confront the realities of their finances, but they were grateful to have Emily guiding them through the process. Emily began by walking them through their current income and expenses, pointing out areas where they could make adjustments.

"The first step is creating a budget that you can stick to. It's important that this budget is realistic and allows for some flexibility, so you don't feel too restricted."

She handed them a detailed breakdown of their monthly expenses. "I've categorized everything into essentials—like housing, utilities, groceries, and transportation—and non-essentials, which include things like dining out, entertainment, and subscriptions. Based on your current income, I recommend cutting back on non-essentials by about 20%. That should free up some money to allocate toward your debts."

Lisa nodded, already mentally calculating how they could adjust their lifestyle. "We've already started cooking more at home and cutting back on unnecessary purchases," she said. "I think we can definitely manage a 20% reduction."

"Great," Emily said encouragingly. "Now, let's talk about your debts. You've been making minimum payments on your credit cards, which is fine, but we need to start chipping away at those balances to avoid accumulating more interest."

She outlined a debt repayment strategy, focusing on the avalanche method, which prioritized paying off the highest interest debt first. "By tackling the most expensive debts first, you'll save more in the long run. We'll allocate any extra funds from your budget to pay down these debts faster."

Alex looked at the plan, feeling a wave of determination. "This makes sense," he said. "We've been so overwhelmed by everything that we didn't know where to start. But having a clear plan like this… it feels doable."

Emily smiled, sensing his resolve. "That's the key—one step at a time. And remember, it's not just about paying off debt. It's about building better habits that will keep you financially stable in the future."

She then discussed the importance of an emergency fund, even if it meant starting small. "Setting aside a little each month, even just $50 or $100, will give you a cushion for unexpected expenses. It might seem difficult now, but it's an essential part of long-term financial health."

Lisa listened intently, making notes. "We can start with that," she said. "It might take time, but we'll get there."

Emily continued to offer practical tips, like setting up automatic transfers into a savings account, using cash for discretionary spending to stay within budget, and regularly reviewing their finances to stay on track.

By the end of the meeting, Alex and Lisa felt a sense of clarity they hadn't had in months. They left Emily's office with a binder full of detailed plans and strategies, but more importantly, with a renewed sense of hope.

As they walked to their car, Lisa linked her arm through Alex's. "I feel like we can actually do this," she said, a small smile playing on her lips. "We've got a plan, we're working together… it's starting to feel like we're moving forward."

Alex nodded, feeling the same. "We are moving forward. And this time, we're doing it the right way. No more avoiding, no more hoping things will just work out. We're taking control."

The drive home was quiet, but the silence was filled with a shared resolve. They were in this together—rebuilding not just their finances, but their trust, their partnership, and their future. When they arrived home, they sat down at the kitchen table, opened the binder, and began laying out the steps they would take. It wasn't just about numbers; it was about the life they wanted to build—one of stability, trust, and mutual support. As they worked side by side, mapping out their financial recovery, Alex couldn't help but feel a sense of gratitude. They had come a long way from the despair of losing his job and the betrayal that had nearly torn them apart. Now, they were on the same team, fighting for their future. The evening ended with them sitting on the porch, watching the stars come out. Lisa rested her head on Alex's shoulder, and he wrapped an arm around her, holding her close.

"We've got this," she whispered, her voice filled with quiet confidence.

"Yeah," Alex replied, feeling that confidence in his own heart. "We do."

And as they sat there together, under the vast night sky, they knew that they were ready for whatever challenges lay ahead. With a plan in place and their bond growing stronger every day, they were not just surviving—they were beginning to thrive.

# CHAPTER 7

The days grew longer as summer approached, bringing with it a sense of renewal. Alex found himself more at ease than he had been in months, thanks to the progress he and Lisa were making both financially and emotionally. The budgeting plan Emily had set up was in full swing, and although there were still challenges, they were managing their debts and even setting aside a small emergency fund. But something in Alex still felt restless. While his part-time job at the grocery store provided some income, he knew it wasn't a long-term solution. He missed the sense of purpose and fulfillment that came from having a career. He knew it was time to start exploring new opportunities.

One Saturday morning, after dropping Emma off at a friend's house, Alex decided to attend a local networking event he'd seen advertised online. It was being held at a nearby community center, a casual affair for professionals looking to connect and explore job opportunities.

Alex arrived early, feeling a mix of nerves and determination. The room was filled with people of all ages, some in suits, others in business-casual attire. He grabbed a name tag and a cup of coffee, then scanned the room, looking for a familiar face. He didn't see anyone he knew, but the energy in the room was positive, and he felt a glimmer of hope. He spent the next couple of hours introducing himself to various people, exchanging business cards, and discussing his background. Some of the conversations were promising; others felt like dead ends. But overall, Alex left the event feeling more connected to the professional world than he had in a long time.

In the days that followed, Alex started exploring online platforms more seriously. He updated his LinkedIn profile, began reaching out to old colleagues, and signed up for several online job boards. He was determined to cast a wide net, knowing that finding the right opportunity might take time. One afternoon, while scrolling through job listings, Alex came across an advertisement for a small business incubator in the area. They were offering support and resources for people interested in starting their own businesses. The idea sparked something in Alex. He had always loved working with his hands, and before life had gotten so complicated, he had enjoyed woodworking as a hobby. The thought of turning that passion into a business had crossed his mind more than once.

With Lisa's encouragement, Alex decided to attend one of the incubator's workshops. The session was focused on how to turn a hobby into a profitable side hustle, and as he listened to the speaker talk about the basics of starting a small business, he felt a flicker of excitement. After the workshop, Alex approached the speaker, a seasoned entrepreneur named Mark, who had started his own woodworking business years ago. They talked for a while, and Mark offered to meet with Alex one-on-one to discuss his ideas and provide some guidance. A week later, Alex found himself in Mark's workshop, surrounded by the rich scent of wood and the sound of tools at work. They spent the afternoon discussing the ins and outs of starting a woodworking business, from sourcing materials to marketing and pricing. Mark was encouraging, offering practical advice and even connecting Alex with a few suppliers.

That evening, Alex sat down with Lisa to discuss the idea in more detail. "I think I want to give this a try," he said, his voice tinged with both excitement and apprehension. "I know it won't be easy, and it'll take time to build, but... I think this could be something real."

Lisa listened carefully, her face thoughtful. "It sounds like you're passionate about it," she said after a moment. "And if this is what you want to do, I'm behind you 100%. We'll figure it out together."

With Lisa's support, Alex decided to move forward. He started small, setting up a workshop in their garage and spending his evenings and weekends working on various pieces—tables, chairs, shelves, and other custom items. He set up an online store, taking care to photograph his work from the best angles, and began posting his products on social media. To his surprise and delight, the response was positive. Friends and family were his first customers, and soon, word began to spread. Orders trickled in slowly at first, but as the weeks passed, they started to pick up. Each sale, no matter how small, filled Alex with a renewed sense of purpose. The positive feedback he received from customers was encouraging. They praised the quality of his craftsmanship, the attention to detail, and the personal touch he put into every piece. For the first time in a long while, Alex felt truly proud of the work he was doing. One evening, after a particularly successful week of sales, Alex sat down in his workshop, reflecting on how far he had come. The business was still in its early stages, but it was growing, and more importantly, it was giving him back a sense of direction that he had lost.

His thoughts turned to Pastor John and the conversations they had shared about purpose and faith. Alex had been praying more, seeking guidance not just for his business, but for his life as a whole. The words of the Bible had started to resonate with him on a deeper level, offering comfort and strength in ways he hadn't expected. As his business grew, so did his spiritual life. Alex found himself spending more time in prayer, not just asking for help, but giving thanks for the blessings he was beginning to see in his life. He started each day with a few moments of quiet reflection, reading passages from the Bible that spoke to him and carrying those words with him throughout the day.

One verse, in particular, stood out to him: "Whatever you do, work at it with all your heart, as working for the Lord, not for human masters." (Colossians 3:23) These words became his mantra, guiding him as he poured his heart into his work, knowing that his efforts were part of a larger purpose. The sense of fulfillment Alex felt was different from anything he had experienced before. It wasn't just about financial success; it was about finding meaning in the everyday tasks, in the simple act of creating something with his hands, and in knowing that he was on a path that aligned with his faith.

Alex's growing confidence and spiritual grounding began to reflect in other areas of his life as well. His relationship with Lisa continued to strengthen, built on the foundation of trust and shared goals they had been rebuilding. Their conversations were deeper, more open, and they found themselves laughing more, enjoying the small moments of life together. Even Emma noticed the change in her parents. The tension that had once filled their home was gone, replaced by a sense of unity and love that she had missed. She began spending more time with them, joining in on family dinners and even helping out in the workshop when she had time.

As the chapter of their lives that had been filled with so much struggle slowly started to close, Alex and Lisa began to look forward with cautious optimism. They knew there would still be challenges ahead, but they also knew they had the strength to face them together, grounded in their faith and their renewed sense of purpose. And as Alex knelt beside his bed one night, offering up a prayer of gratitude, he felt a deep sense of peace. He was on the right path—a path that was leading him toward healing, growth, and new opportunities that were waiting just beyond the horizon.

The summer days passed in a blur of sawdust and sunlight as Alex's small woodworking business steadily grew. What had started as a hobby and a side hustle was quickly turning into something more substantial. His online store began receiving more traffic, and the word-of-mouth buzz in town was unmistakable. People appreciated the quality of his work, and his custom pieces were becoming sought-after items in the community. One weekend, a local newspaper ran a feature on his business, highlighting his journey from corporate layoff to successful entrepreneur. The article painted Alex as a symbol of resilience, and soon after, orders began pouring in. Customers from neighboring towns and even out-of-state started reaching out, eager to purchase one-of-a-kind pieces crafted by Alex's hands. With the influx of orders, Alex found himself working late into the night, balancing the demands of his growing business with his responsibilities at home. Lisa and Emma pitched in when they could—Lisa managing the books and Emma helping with packaging and shipping. The garage, once a simple workshop, was now a hive of activity, filled with the hum of tools and the scent of freshly cut wood.

Despite the long hours, Alex felt a deep sense of fulfillment. He was building something meaningful, not just for himself but for his family. Each piece he crafted was a testament to his hard work, faith, and the support of those around him.

One evening, as Alex was sorting through emails, he noticed a message from an unfamiliar sender. The subject line read, "Investment Opportunity—Potential Partnership."

Curious, he clicked on it. The email was from someone named Richard Caldwell, an angel investor based in a nearby city. Richard explained that he had come across the article in the local newspaper and had been following Alex's business ever since. He was impressed by the quality of Alex's work and the story behind his business. Richard went on to say that he was interested in discussing a potential investment, which could help Alex expand his operations, reach a broader market, and take his business to the next level. Alex sat back in his chair, staring at the screen. The idea of having an investor was both exciting and intimidating. It could mean more resources, the ability to hire additional help, and even moving into a larger workshop space. But it also meant giving up some control and possibly taking on more risk. Before making any decisions, Alex knew he needed advice. He quickly drafted a reply to Richard, thanking him for his interest and suggesting that they arrange a meeting to discuss the details. Then, he turned to the one person who had been guiding them through their financial journey—Emily.

The next morning, Alex called Emily and explained the situation. "I'm not sure what to do," he admitted. "This could be a great opportunity, but I don't want to rush into anything without understanding the full implications."

Emily listened carefully before responding. "You're right to be cautious, Alex. An investment can be a fantastic way to grow your business, but it's important to go into it with your eyes wide open. Why don't we set up a meeting to go over the offer? We can discuss the pros and cons, and I can help you prepare for the conversation with Richard."

They arranged to meet later that week at Emily's office. When the day came, Alex felt a mixture of excitement and nerves as he walked in, carrying a folder filled with all the information he had about his business, including financial statements, growth projections, and the email from Richard. Emily greeted him warmly and led him to a conference room where they spread out the documents on the table.

"Let's start by going over your business as it stands now," she suggested. "We'll look at your current financials, your growth potential, and what kind of investment you might need to reach your goals."

For the next hour, they reviewed the details. Emily was thorough, asking questions about Alex's vision for the business, his long-term goals, and how much control he was willing to relinquish to an investor.

"Richard's email is very positive, but we need to make sure you fully understand what any partnership might entail," Emily explained. "Typically, an investor would expect some equity in the business, meaning they would own a portion of it and have a say in how it's run. The key is finding a balance between getting the support you need and maintaining enough control to keep the business aligned with your vision."

Alex nodded, appreciating Emily's clear and practical approach. They discussed potential scenarios, including what would happen if the business grew rapidly or, conversely, if it faced challenges. Emily also suggested that they bring in a lawyer to review any contracts and ensure that Alex's interests were protected.

By the end of the meeting, Alex felt more prepared and confident about the next steps. Emily had helped him clarify his priorities and understand what questions to ask during his meeting with Richard.

"Remember, Alex," Emily said as they wrapped up, "this is your business, and you've built it with your hard work and dedication. Don't be afraid to negotiate and make sure any partnership is truly beneficial for you and your family."

Alex thanked her, feeling a sense of relief that he wasn't going into this alone. He had a plan, he knew what to look out for, and most importantly, he had a team of people—Lisa, Emma, Emily, and even Pastor John—who supported him.

As he drove home, Alex's mind buzzed with possibilities. The meeting with Richard was set for the following week, and while there were still uncertainties, Alex felt ready to face them. He knew that whatever happened, he was moving forward on a path that was not only promising but also grounded in the values and faith that had carried him through the toughest times.

Back home, he shared everything with Lisa, who listened intently, her expression thoughtful. "This could be big," she said, her eyes reflecting the same mixture of excitement and caution that Alex felt. "But like Emily said, we need to make sure it's the right move for us."

Alex nodded, grateful once again for the partnership he and Lisa had rebuilt. "We'll take it one step at a time," he said, reaching for her hand. "And we'll do it together."

With the meeting with Richard just days away, Alex focused on preparing himself. He revisited his goals, his vision for the future, and most importantly, the values that would guide his decisions. Whatever came next, Alex knew he was ready—ready to embrace new opportunities, face new challenges, and continue building the life he and his family had worked so hard to reclaim.

# CHAPTER 8

The following months marked a turning point in Alex's life, as the small steps he had taken began to coalesce into something tangible. His business, initially a modest side hustle born out of desperation, began to grow in ways he hadn't anticipated. The simple joy of crafting handmade furniture in his garage, a hobby that had once been an escape from the pressures of life, was now becoming a beacon of hope and stability. Orders started to pour in, first from local customers who appreciated the craftsmanship and care Alex put into his work. Then, as word spread through social media and positive reviews, the demand began to expand beyond their small town. It wasn't long before Alex found himself working long hours, trying to keep up with the influx of requests. The garage, once a quiet place of solitude, was now bustling with activity. Lisa watched as Alex's spirits lifted with each new order. The sight of him engaged in his work, his hands steady as they shaped wood into beautiful, functional pieces, brought a sense of peace back into their home. She helped where she could, handling the business's finances and logistics, but mostly, she stood back, allowing Alex to find his rhythm again.

One evening, after a particularly busy day, Alex sat down with Lisa at the kitchen table, the day's receipts and orders spread out before them. The business was doing well—better than they had dared to hope. But with the success came new challenges, and the decisions they now faced were critical.

They sat together, going over their options. One of the main decisions they faced was whether to reinvest in the business, expanding it further, or to play it safe, putting more money aside for Emma's education and their own financial security. It was a delicate balance—risk versus stability.

"I don't want to lose what we've gained," Alex said, his voice thoughtful. "But I also don't want to let fear hold us back."

Lisa nodded in agreement. "We've come so far, and we need to be smart about this. But we also need to trust that we can make the right decisions together."

After hours of discussion, they decided to reinvest a portion of the profits into the business, expanding the workshop and hiring a part-time assistant to help with the growing workload. The rest would be carefully allocated to savings and Emma's college fund, ensuring they were building a solid foundation for the future. As they finalized their plan, Alex felt a deep sense of satisfaction. The success of the business wasn't just about financial stability—it was about rebuilding his life, his sense of purpose, and his family's future. The decisions they were making now were a testament to the journey they had been on, the struggles they had overcome, and the hope that had slowly been rekindled in their lives.

As the business grew, so did Alex's sense of spiritual fulfillment. Pastor John's guidance had been instrumental in helping him navigate the dark days, and now, with the business flourishing, Alex felt a renewed sense of gratitude. He began to see his success not just as a result of his hard work, but as a gift—a second chance at life that he was determined not to waste.

One Sunday, after service, Alex approached Pastor John. "I've been thinking a lot about what you said, about finding meaning beyond just financial success," Alex began. "I want to do more, to give back in some way."

Pastor John smiled warmly. "That's wonderful, Alex. There's always a way to use your gifts to help others. What did you have in mind?"

Alex thought for a moment before replying. "I want to start donating a portion of the profits from the business to the church's community programs. I've been blessed, and I want to make sure that blessing is passed on."

Pastor John's eyes lit up. "That's a generous offer, Alex. I'm sure it will make a real difference in the lives of those who need it most."

The decision to give back brought Alex a deep sense of peace. It was a way of acknowledging the journey he had been on, the challenges he had faced, and the support he had received. It also reinforced the idea that his success was not just for him and his family, but for the community that had helped him find his way.

In the weeks that followed, Alex became more involved in the church's charity initiatives. He volunteered his time, helping to organize events and fundraisers, and donated pieces of furniture to families in need. The work was fulfilling in a way that went beyond financial gain—it was about making a tangible difference in the lives of others. One day, as Alex was delivering a handcrafted dining table to a family who had lost their home in a fire, he was struck by the gratitude in their eyes. The father of the family, a man who had lost almost everything, shook Alex's hand with tears in his eyes.

"This means more to us than you could ever know," the man said, his voice thick with emotion. "Thank you, from the bottom of our hearts."

As Alex drove home that day, he felt a profound sense of purpose. The road to this point had been long and fraught with challenges, but it had led him to a place of deep spiritual and emotional fulfillment. The success of his business was important, but the ability to give back, to help others rebuild their lives, was what truly mattered.

The financial growth of Alex's business had brought a new level of stability to his life, both materially and spiritually. The garage, now a fully equipped workshop, was a testament to the journey he had been on—a place of creation and renewal, where he had found a way to rebuild his life from the ground up. At home, the atmosphere was lighter. The tension that had once filled every room had been replaced with a sense of peace and optimism. Alex and

Lisa were closer than they had been in years, their relationship strengthened by the trials they had endured together. Emma, too, seemed happier, her parents' renewed connection providing a sense of security.

One evening, as they sat together at the dinner table, Alex looked around at his family, a deep sense of gratitude welling up inside him. The road ahead would still have its challenges, but for the first time in a long time, he felt truly prepared to face whatever came their way. As the night drew to a close, Alex stepped out onto the porch, taking in the cool evening air. He looked up at the stars, feeling a quiet sense of contentment. The journey had been long, and the struggles had been many, but he had found his way back— back to his family, back to his faith, and back to a life filled with purpose and meaning.

With the future spread out before him like the vast night sky, Alex knew that he was ready. Ready to face whatever came next, with the confidence that, no matter what, he would be able to answer the question that had once filled him with dread: "What you gonna do now?" His answer, now, was simple—he would keep moving forward, with faith, love, and determination guiding his way.

With the business thriving, it became clear to Alex and Lisa that they could no longer manage everything on their own. The orders were coming in faster than Alex could fulfill them, and the administrative tasks were beginning to pile up, consuming more of Lisa's time. It was time to take the next step.

One evening, after another long day in the workshop, Alex sat down with Lisa at the kitchen table. They had just finished dinner, and Emma had gone up to her room to study. The house was quiet, the kind of peaceful calm that had become a welcome norm in their lives again.

"We need help," Alex said, his tone serious but calm. "I can't keep up with the demand, and I don't want to start turning down orders. I think it's time we hired someone."

Lisa nodded in agreement, having anticipated this conversation. "I've been thinking the same thing. We can't keep running this as just the two of us, not with how much we've grown. But we have to be smart about it. We need someone who's reliable, and who's going to fit in well with us."

They talked late into the night, discussing what they were looking for in a potential assistant. They needed someone who was willing to learn, who had a strong work ethic, and who could be trusted to handle both the physical demands of the workshop and some of the basic administrative tasks. It wasn't just about finding an employee—it was about finding someone who could be a part of their growing business, someone who could share in their vision. The next morning, Lisa drafted a job vacancy memo. It was simple but clear, outlining the responsibilities of the position and the qualities they were looking for. They decided to post it on local job boards, social media, and at the community center, hoping to attract candidates who were eager to work with their hands and be a part of something meaningful.

Over the next week, the applications started coming in. At first, it was just a trickle, but soon enough, Alex and Lisa found themselves with a sizable stack of resumes to sift through. They spent their evenings together, going over each one, discussing the merits of the various candidates.

"This one seems promising," Lisa said, holding up a resume from a young man with a background in carpentry. "He's got some experience, and it looks like he's eager to learn more."

Alex nodded, glancing over the resume. "He could be a good fit. But I also want to give a chance to someone who might not have as much experience but has the right attitude. We can teach skills, but we can't teach work ethic."

They continued sorting through the applications, creating two piles—one for those who seemed like a strong fit and another for those who, while qualified, didn't quite align with what they were looking for. Eventually, they narrowed it down to seven candidates who they felt had the potential to be a good match for their business.

Alex was both nervous and excited as he prepared for the interviews. It was the first time he would be hiring someone for his business, and he wanted to make sure he got it right. Lisa had helped him prepare a list of questions that would not only assess the candidates' skills but also gauge their enthusiasm and alignment with the values of the business. One by one, the candidates came to the workshop for their interviews. Alex greeted each of them personally, showing them around and explaining the work that he did. The conversations were casual but informative, with Alex paying close attention to how each candidate responded to the questions and how they carried themselves.

By the end of the day, he felt a sense of accomplishment. He had met some genuinely good people, and he was confident that one of them would be the right fit for the job. But one candidate stood out among the rest. His name was Tyler, a young man just out of high school. He had little formal experience but spoke with a passion and sincerity that caught Alex's attention. Tyler had grown up in a family that valued hard work, and though he had dabbled in various odd jobs, he had never found something that truly resonated with him—until now.

"I've always wanted to work with my hands," Tyler had said during the interview, his eyes bright with excitement. "There's something about creating something real, something tangible, that just feels right. I don't have a lot of experience, but I'm eager to learn. I'm willing to do whatever it takes to prove myself."

Alex could see a reflection of his younger self in Tyler's enthusiasm and honesty. He remembered what it was like to be young and eager, searching for something meaningful to do with his life. After the interviews were over, Alex sat down with Lisa to discuss the candidates, but his mind kept coming back to Tyler.

"I think Tyler's the one," Alex said finally, his decision firm. "He may not have the most experience, but he's got the drive, and I can teach him the rest. Plus, he's got that spark—the one you can't fake."

Lisa smiled, nodding in agreement. "I had a feeling you'd pick him. I think he'll be a great addition."

The next day, Alex called Tyler with the news. He could hear the excitement in Tyler's voice as he accepted the offer, grateful for the opportunity. They agreed on a start date, and Alex hung up the phone feeling a deep sense of satisfaction. It wasn't just about growing the business anymore; it was about passing on his knowledge, mentoring someone, and building something bigger than himself. When Tyler arrived for his first day, Alex took him under his wing, showing him the ropes and teaching him the intricacies of woodworking. Tyler was a quick learner, eager to soak up everything Alex had to offer. Over time, the two developed a strong working relationship, built on mutual respect and a shared passion for the craft. As the weeks passed, the workshop hummed with new energy. Tyler's presence allowed Alex to take on more projects, and the business continued to grow. But more importantly, Alex found a renewed sense of purpose in teaching and guiding someone who reminded him so much of himself.

As the business continued to grow, Alex found himself grappling with questions that went beyond the day-to-day operations of his workshop. The financial success was undeniable— orders were steadily increasing, and the business was thriving in ways he hadn't imagined when he first started. But as the numbers in his bank account rose, so did a nagging sense of emptiness, a feeling that there was more to this journey than just profits and expansion. One evening, after a particularly long day in the workshop, Alex decided to visit Pastor John. He hadn't had a chance to catch up with him in a while, and he felt the need to talk to someone who could help him make sense of the thoughts swirling in his mind. After calling ahead, he drove to the church and found Pastor John in his office, surrounded by books and papers.

"Alex!" Pastor John greeted him warmly, rising from his desk to embrace him. "It's good to see you. How have you been?"

"I've been good," Alex replied, smiling as he took a seat across from Pastor John. "The business is doing really well—better than I ever expected, honestly. But that's actually why I'm here. I've been doing a lot of thinking lately, and I'm starting to wonder if I'm missing something."

Pastor John leaned forward, his expression thoughtful. "Tell me more. What's on your mind?"

Alex sighed, running a hand through his hair as he tried to find the right words. "It's just... everything is going well financially. We're not struggling like we were before, and I'm grateful for that. But I keep asking myself, what's the point of all this? Is it just about making money? Because if that's all it is, then I feel like I'm missing something important."

Pastor John nodded slowly, understanding the weight of Alex's question. "It's not uncommon to feel that way, especially when you've achieved the kind of success you have. The world often tells us that success is measured in dollars and possessions, but as you're discovering, there's more to life than just financial gain."

Alex looked up, meeting Pastor John's eyes. "I don't want to lose sight of what really matters. I started this business because I needed to rebuild my life after everything fell apart. It gave me purpose, and it helped me reconnect with Lisa and with God. But now that things are going well, I'm worried that I'm getting too caught up in the numbers, in the growth, and forgetting why I started in the first place."

Pastor John smiled gently, leaning back in his chair. "It's a good thing that you're asking these questions, Alex. It shows that you're not just focused on the material, but on the spiritual and emotional aspects of your life as well. Success, true success, is about more than just what we accumulate. It's about how we live our lives, the impact we have on others, and the legacy we leave behind."

Alex nodded, feeling a sense of clarity begin to emerge. "I've been thinking about that too—about how I can use this success to help others. Tyler, the young man I just hired, has reminded me of how important it is to mentor and guide others, just like you and others did for me. I want to make sure that this business isn't just about making money, but about giving back, about helping others find their way."

"That's exactly the kind of thinking that will lead you to a more fulfilling and meaningful life," Pastor John said, his voice warm with encouragement. "You've been blessed with success, but those blessings come with a responsibility. By using your gifts to help others, to lift them up and guide them, you're aligning your work with a higher purpose."

Alex felt a deep sense of peace as he listened to Pastor John's words. It was as if the pieces of the puzzle were finally falling into place, revealing a picture that was richer and more complex than he had imagined.

"Thank you, Pastor John," Alex said, his voice filled with gratitude. "I think I just needed to hear that. It's easy to get lost in the day-to-day and forget why we're doing all of this. But I don't want to lose sight of what really matters—my family, my faith, and the people I can help along the way."

Pastor John reached across the desk, placing a hand on Alex's shoulder. "You're on the right path, Alex. Keep seeking that balance, and you'll find that success isn't just about what you have, but about who you are and how you live your life."

As Alex left the church that evening, he felt a renewed sense of purpose. The questions that had been troubling him no longer seemed daunting; instead, they felt like opportunities to grow, to deepen his faith, and to make a positive impact on the world around him. And as he drove home, the familiar landscape passing by, he knew that this journey was far from over—there was still so much more to discover, so much more to give.

# CHAPTER 9

The conversation with Pastor John lingered in Alex's mind long after he left the church. The clarity he had gained that evening began to shape his thoughts and actions in the days that followed. He knew that his business success had given him a platform, an opportunity to do more than just provide for his family—it had given him a chance to make a real difference in the lives of others. The next morning, as Alex stood in the workshop, surrounded by the smell of freshly cut wood and the hum of machinery, he couldn't shake the feeling that it was time to act on the inspiration he had felt. The words of Pastor John echoed in his mind: "Success isn't just about what you have, but about who you are and how you live your life."

After mulling it over for a few days, Alex approached Lisa with the idea one evening as they sat together on the porch, watching the sunset paint the sky in shades of orange and pink.

"I've been thinking a lot about what Pastor John said," Alex began, his voice contemplative. "About using our success to help others. I think we should start donating a portion of the business's profits to the church's community programs."

Lisa looked at him, her eyes reflecting the same sunset hues. She smiled, nodding in agreement. "I think that's a wonderful idea, Alex. We've been blessed, and it's only right that we give back. The church's programs have helped so many people, including us, when we needed it the most."

Alex felt a surge of gratitude for Lisa's unwavering support. He had been fortunate to have her by his side, through all the ups and downs. "I want to make sure that we're not just growing this business for ourselves, but for the good we can do with it. I don't want to forget what really matters."

Together, they decided on a percentage of the profits to donate each month. It was a meaningful amount, enough to make a real impact on the church's programs while still allowing the business to continue growing and supporting their family. Alex felt a sense of fulfillment as they made the decision, knowing that this was the right path for them.

The following Sunday, Alex approached Pastor John after the service. The church was alive with the usual post-service chatter, but Alex was focused on the conversation he needed to have.

"Pastor John, can I talk to you for a minute?" Alex asked, catching him as he greeted other members of the congregation.

"Of course, Alex," Pastor John replied with a warm smile. He led Alex to a quieter corner of the church. "What's on your mind?"

Alex explained his plan to donate a portion of his business's profits to the church's community programs. As he spoke, Pastor John's smile widened, and he nodded in approval.

"That's incredibly generous, Alex," Pastor John said. "Your support will make a huge difference in the lives of so many people. We've been able to do a lot with what we have, but with your contribution, we can expand our programs, reach more people, and provide even more support to those in need."

Hearing this filled Alex with a sense of purpose and satisfaction. "I just want to give back, Pastor. The church and the community have been there for me when I needed it most, and I want to do the same for others."

Pastor John placed a hand on Alex's shoulder, his eyes filled with gratitude. "You're doing more than just giving back, Alex. You're setting an example, showing others that success isn't just about what you gain, but about what you give. I'm proud of you."

As the weeks passed, Alex's decision to donate part of his profits became a regular part of his business operations. Each month, he wrote a check to the church, knowing that the money was going towards programs that fed the hungry, provided shelter for the homeless, and offered counseling and support to those going through difficult times.

The act of giving brought a new dimension to his work. It wasn't just about making furniture anymore; it was about creating something that could serve a higher purpose. The more he gave, the more fulfilled he felt, and this fulfillment began to ripple out into other areas of his life. He noticed a renewed sense of peace in his home, a deeper connection with Lisa, and an even stronger bond with the people around him.

Tyler, the young assistant he had hired, noticed the change too. One day, as they were working on a particularly large order, Tyler paused and looked at Alex.

"Mr. Hamilton," Tyler began, hesitating slightly as he chose his words, "I've been hearing from some folks at the church about the donations you've been making. I just wanted to say... it's really inspiring. You didn't have to do that, but you did. It's made me think a lot about what I want to do with my life, and how I can make a difference too."

Alex smiled, feeling a deep sense of pride. "Thank you, Tyler. I think we all have a responsibility to do what we can, to give back in whatever way we're able. It doesn't always have to be money—sometimes it's our time, our skills, or just being there for someone when they need it. But whatever it is, it's important to do it."

Tyler nodded, clearly taking Alex's words to heart. "I want to help too, Mr. Hamilton. Maybe I can volunteer at the church or something. I'm not sure yet, but I want to start making a difference, even in small ways."

Alex felt his heart swell with gratitude. This was exactly what he had hoped for—not just to give back himself, but to inspire others to do the same. It was a reminder that success wasn't just about the here and now; it was about creating a legacy that could endure, a ripple effect that could touch lives far beyond his own.

As they continued working, Alex couldn't help but feel that he was on the right path. The business was growing, yes, but more importantly, so was his understanding of what it meant to live a life of purpose. The journey was far from over, but for the first time in a long time, Alex felt truly at peace with where he was and where he was going.

# CHAPTER 10

As the weeks turned into months, the rhythm of Alex's life began to stabilize. His business continued to grow steadily, and the sense of purpose he had found through giving back enriched every aspect of his daily routine. But just as he was starting to feel like he had everything under control, life, as it often does, threw a new challenge his way.

One afternoon, as Alex was finishing up a custom order in the workshop, his phone buzzed with a call from his sister, Sarah. The concern in her voice was palpable even before she spoke.

"Alex, it's Mom and Dad," she began, her words tinged with worry. "Dad's health has been declining faster than we expected. I think we need to start planning for the worst."

The news hit Alex like a punch to the gut. His parents, who had always been pillars of strength in his life, were now facing the inevitable reality of aging. His father, once a strong and vigorous man, was now frail and in need of constant care. His mother, too, was struggling, her energy drained by the relentless demands of caregiving.

"I'll be there as soon as I can," Alex replied, his voice steady despite the turmoil he felt inside.

The drive to his parents' house was a blur of emotions. Memories of his father teaching him to build furniture, of his mother's comforting presence in times of trouble, flooded his mind. As he pulled into the driveway, he braced himself for what awaited inside.

His father, Robert, was sitting in his favorite chair by the window, gazing out at the backyard where he had once spent countless hours tending to the garden. But now, he looked tired, his once-bright eyes dimmed by illness. His mother, Margaret, was bustling around the kitchen, but even from a distance, Alex could see the exhaustion etched on her face.

"Hey, Dad," Alex greeted as he walked in, trying to keep his tone light. "How are you feeling today?"

Robert turned his head slowly, a small smile tugging at the corners of his mouth. "Just taking it one day at a time, son. How's that business of yours coming along?"

"It's going well," Alex replied, sitting down next to his father. "But I'm more worried about you right now."

Robert waved his hand dismissively. "Don't you go worrying about me. I've had a good run. But I'm glad you're here. Your mother could use the help."

As the day went on, Alex helped his mother with the household chores, taking some of the burden off her shoulders. They talked about the logistics of care, about hiring help, and about the difficult decisions that lay ahead. But amidst the practical discussions, there was an unspoken understanding that this was a turning point, a moment when roles were being reversed, and the child was becoming the caregiver.

That evening, after settling his father into bed, Alex sat down with his mother in the living room. The house was quiet, the only sound was the ticking of the clock on the mantle.

"Mom, I've been thinking," Alex began, choosing his words carefully. "I want to be here more often, to help out with Dad. I can't imagine how hard this has been for you."

Margaret looked at her son, her eyes filled with a mixture of gratitude and sadness. "I appreciate that, Alex. But I know you have your own family and your business to take care of. I don't want to be a burden."

"You're not a burden," Alex said firmly. "You and Dad have done so much for me. It's my turn to be there for you. We'll figure it out together."

Margaret reached out and took his hand, squeezing it gently. "You've grown into such a good man, Alex. Your father and I are so proud of you."

They sat in silence for a while, the weight of their shared burdens filling the space between them. But it was a comfortable silence, one that spoke of love, of family, and of the unbreakable bonds that held them together. Over the next few weeks, Alex found himself juggling his responsibilities in ways he hadn't anticipated. He spent more time at his parents' house, helping with his father's care and providing emotional support to his mother. The experience was both draining and fulfilling, pushing him to new levels of patience and compassion. At the same time, he continued to manage his business, often working late into the night to keep up with orders and maintain the momentum he had built. The challenge was daunting, but Alex found strength in the knowledge that he was doing what was right, that he was honoring his parents in their time of need.

One evening, after a particularly exhausting day, Alex returned home to find Lisa and Emma waiting for him in the living room. The sight of them, his anchors in this storm, brought a smile to his tired face.

"Hey, you two," Alex greeted, his voice warm despite his fatigue. "What's going on?"

"We wanted to talk to you about something," Lisa said, her tone gentle but serious. "We know you've been under a lot of pressure lately, with the business and your parents. And we just want you to know that we're here for you."

Emma nodded, her teenage face full of concern. "Yeah, Dad. We want to help. Maybe we can take on more responsibilities around the house, or even help out with Grandpa and Grandma."

Alex's heart swelled with pride and gratitude. "You don't know how much that means to me," he said, his voice thick with emotion. "I've been trying to keep everything together, but it's been hard. Knowing that I have you both by my side makes all the difference."

Together, they talked about how they could manage the challenges ahead as a family. They discussed schedules, responsibilities, and how they could support one another during this difficult time. It was a conversation that deepened their bond, reinforcing the sense of unity that had carried them through so many other trials.

Amidst the whirlwind of responsibilities, Alex continued to find solace in his faith. He turned to prayer more often, seeking guidance and strength in the face of the many demands on his time and energy. His conversations with Pastor John became more frequent, as he sought advice on how to balance his duties as a son, a husband, and a father.

One Sunday after church, Alex found himself alone with Pastor John in the sanctuary, the morning light streaming through the stained-glass windows.

"Pastor, I've been feeling overwhelmed lately," Alex admitted, his voice heavy with the weight of his emotions. "There's so much to do, and I'm afraid I'm going to let someone down. Whether it's my parents, my family, or my business… it feels like there's not enough of me to go around."

Pastor John listened carefully, his expression compassionate. "Alex, it's natural to feel that way when you're carrying so many responsibilities. But remember, you're not alone in this. You have your family, your community, and most importantly, you have God's strength to lean on. You don't have to carry this burden by yourself."

Alex nodded, taking in the pastor's words. "I know, but it's hard to let go, to trust that everything will work out."

"It's not about letting go, but about letting God in," Pastor John said gently. "You're doing everything you can, and that's enough. Trust in God's plan, and let Him guide you through this. You've come so far, Alex, and you've grown so much. Keep that faith strong, and you'll find the strength to carry on."

As Alex drove home that day, he reflected on Pastor John's words. He realized that while he couldn't do everything perfectly, he could do his best, and that had to be enough. He had to trust in the support of his family, his friends, and his faith to help him through. Gradually, he found a new balance, one that allowed him to care for his parents while still nurturing his own family and business. It wasn't easy, and there were days when he felt stretched to his limit, but he took each day as it came, relying on the strength of his loved ones and the peace he found in his faith. In caring for his father, Alex discovered a new depth to their relationship, one that transcended the years of distance and misunderstandings. They talked more openly, sharing stories and memories, and even in his weakened state, Robert offered his son wisdom and encouragement. It was a healing process for both of them, a way to mend old wounds and create new bonds.

And as Alex continued to give back to his community through his business, he found that the more he gave, the more he received in return—not just in financial success, but in the form of friendships, support, and a deepening sense of purpose.

# CHAPTER 11

As the days turned into weeks, Alex found himself reflecting more deeply on the purpose of his life. The challenges of balancing his business, caring for his parents, and nurturing his own family had pushed him to the brink, yet they had also led him to discover a new sense of meaning. After a long day of work and caregiving, Alex sat on the porch of his parents' home, watching the sun dip below the horizon. The sky was painted in hues of orange and pink, and the air was cool and calm. It was one of those rare moments of peace, where everything felt still and quiet. Alex thought back to the conversation he had with Pastor John about success. In the past, he had measured his worth by his career achievements, by the promotions he had earned, and by the financial stability he had provided for his family. But now, as he looked back on the path he had taken, he realized that true success was far more complex, far more profound.

Success, he mused, wasn't just about climbing the corporate ladder or accumulating wealth. It was about the impact he made on the lives of those around him. It was about the love he gave, the sacrifices he made, and the way he showed up for the people who depended on him. It was about the legacy he was creating—not through material possessions, but through the relationships he was nurturing and the kindness he was spreading. The more Alex thought about it, the more he realized that his life had taken on a new dimension. By serving his family—by caring for his ailing father, by supporting his mother, by being present for Lisa and Emma—he was fulfilling a purpose far greater than any job title could offer. And through his work in the community, by donating a portion of his profits to the church's programs, by mentoring others who were struggling, he was contributing to something larger than himself. This realization brought a deep sense of fulfillment, one that he hadn't experienced before. For the first time in his life, Alex felt truly content, not because everything was perfect, but because he was living in alignment with his values. He was serving others in a meaningful way, and that, he understood now, was the greatest success of all.

That night, as Alex returned home, he found Lisa in the kitchen, preparing dinner. The smell of her cooking filled the house, and there was a warmth in the air that made him feel at ease.

"Hey," Alex greeted, walking over to her. "Smells great in here."

Lisa smiled, looking up from the stove. "Thanks. I made your favorite—chicken Alfredo. I figured we could all use a nice family dinner tonight."

Alex leaned against the counter, watching her as she stirred the sauce. "I was thinking about something today," he began, his tone thoughtful. "About how we measure success. I used to think it was all about money and career, but now... I'm starting to see it differently."

Lisa turned off the stove and faced him, curiosity in her eyes. "What do you mean?"

"I mean, I've been thinking about how much more fulfilling it is to serve others," Alex explained. "Taking care of Dad, being there for you and Emma, giving back to the community—it's made me realize that success isn't about what we gain, but about what we give. It's about the impact we make, the love we share. And that's something money can't buy."

Lisa's expression softened, and she stepped closer to him, wrapping her arms around his waist. "I've seen the changes in you, Alex. You're more present, more at peace. And it's made a difference for all of us. I'm proud of the man you're becoming."

Her words touched something deep within him, and Alex hugged her tightly, feeling a wave of gratitude wash over him. "I'm just trying to do what's right," he said softly. "For our family, and for everyone who's helped us along the way."

Over the next few weeks, Alex became even more involved in the church's community programs. He volunteered his time, not just his money, helping to organize food drives, mentoring those in the job support group, and even offering workshops on woodworking for anyone interested in learning a new skill. Each time he gave, whether it was a few hours of his time or a donation from his business, he felt a sense of purpose that was both humbling and uplifting. The gratitude he saw in the eyes of those he helped was more rewarding than any paycheck he had ever received. One Saturday morning, as he and Pastor John were setting up tables for a charity event, the pastor looked over at Alex with a knowing smile.

"You've found something here, haven't you?" Pastor John asked, his voice gentle.

Alex paused, thinking about the question. "Yeah, I guess I have," he replied, looking around at the bustling activity of volunteers preparing for the event. "I've found a sense of belonging, a community that I'm proud to be a part of. It's not just about what I can give—it's about being connected to something bigger than myself. It's about making a difference."

Pastor John nodded, his smile deepening. "That's the beauty of service, Alex. It's not just about helping others; it's about finding our own place in the world. When we give of ourselves, we receive so much more in return—wisdom, peace, and a sense of fulfillment that can't be measured by worldly standards."

Alex took those words to heart, carrying them with him as he continued to navigate the challenges of life. Every time he served— whether it was his parents, his family, or his community—he was reminded of the deeper meaning behind his actions. He was reminded that success wasn't about personal gain, but about the love, kindness, and support he could offer to those around him. And as he lay down to sleep each night, Alex felt a profound sense of peace, knowing that he was living a life of purpose. He was no longer just a man trying to rebuild what he had lost—he was a man building something new, something lasting, and something that truly mattered.

# CHAPTER 12

Alex stood in the middle of his workshop, surrounded by stacks of wood, half-finished pieces of furniture, and the hum of productivity. The business he had once started as a desperate side hustle had grown into something far more substantial. Orders were coming in steadily, and he had even expanded his offerings to include custom designs, a move that had attracted a loyal clientele. As the business grew, so did the demands on his time. Yet, Alex found himself more at peace than he had ever been. There was a rhythm to his days now, a balance between work and family, between business and service. And with each piece of furniture he crafted, he felt a deeper connection to his craft and to the people who would eventually bring his work into their homes.

One evening, after another productive day at the workshop, Alex and Lisa sat down at the kitchen table to review their finances. It had become a weekly routine, a habit they had developed to stay on top of their growing business and the household budget.

"Look at this," Lisa said, pointing to a spreadsheet on her laptop. "We're finally ahead on all our bills, and we've started building a decent savings account. We might even be able to start putting away more for Emma's college fund."

Alex nodded, a sense of pride swelling in his chest. "It feels good, doesn't it? Knowing that we're not just getting by anymore, but actually thriving."

Lisa smiled warmly at him. "It feels amazing. And it's all because of the hard work you've put in. You turned this business into something real, something that's providing for our family in ways we never thought possible."

Alex leaned back in his chair, a contemplative expression on his face. "It's funny," he mused. "A year ago, I was so focused on climbing the corporate ladder, on making more money and getting ahead. But now… Now I see that success isn't just about how much we make. It's about the life we're building, the stability we're creating for our family, and the way we're able to give back to our community."

Lisa reached across the table and took his hand. "You've come a long way, Alex. We both have. And I'm so grateful that we've been able to do this together."

They sat in comfortable silence for a few moments, savoring the peace that had settled over their home. The financial struggles that had once consumed them were no longer a constant source of anxiety. They had found a way to manage their money, to invest in their future, and to live within their means—all while growing their business and giving back to those in need.

As the months passed, Alex and Lisa continued to focus on their goals, both personal and professional. They paid off their debts, set aside money for Emma's college fund, and even started exploring the possibility of investing in a rental property—a long-held dream that now seemed within reach. But beyond the financial milestones, Alex found himself drawn more deeply into the spiritual and community aspects of his life. His involvement in the church's programs had become a source of joy and fulfillment, something he looked forward to each week.

On a fine and brisk-looking Saturday, after a particularly busy morning at the church's food bank, Pastor John pulled Alex aside.

"You've been a real blessing to this community, Alex," Pastor John said, his voice filled with warmth and gratitude. "The work you're doing here, the support you're providing—it's making a difference in ways you might not even realize."

Alex smiled modestly, still not entirely comfortable with praise. "I'm just trying to do what feels right. It's not always easy, but it feels good to give back, to be part of something bigger than myself."

Pastor John nodded. "That's the key, isn't it? Finding that balance between providing for our own needs and giving to others. It's something we all struggle with, but you've managed to find a way to integrate it into your life in a meaningful way."

Alex considered this for a moment. "I think it's because I've finally figured out what's truly important to me. It's not about the money, or the status, or even the success of the business. It's about the relationships I'm building, the love I'm sharing with my family, and the way I'm able to help others who are going through tough times."

Pastor John smiled, his eyes twinkling with understanding. "That's the kind of wisdom that can only come from experience, from walking through the fire and coming out the other side. You've been through a lot, Alex, and you've emerged stronger for it."

Alex nodded, feeling a deep sense of affirmation. He had indeed been through a lot—more than he ever thought he could handle. But each challenge, each setback, had taught him something valuable. And now, standing on the other side, he could see how all the pieces had come together to create a life that was rich in meaning and purpose.

With the business thriving and their finances in order, Alex and Lisa began to seriously discuss their long-term goals. One evening, after putting Emma to bed, they sat down in the living room with a stack of papers spread out on the coffee table.

"Okay," Lisa said, picking up a pen. "Let's talk about this investment property idea. I've been doing some research, and there are a few places in town that might be a good fit for us."

Alex leaned forward, looking at the listings she had printed out. "This one looks interesting," he said, pointing to a modest duplex in a quiet neighborhood. "It's not too expensive, and it seems like it could bring in a decent rental income."

Lisa nodded, her expression thoughtful. "It could be a good way to diversify our income, especially now that the business is stable.

Plus, it's something we've always talked about doing—having an investment property as part of our long-term plan."

They spent the next hour discussing the pros and cons of each option, weighing the potential risks and rewards. It was a serious conversation, but one that was filled with excitement and anticipation for the future.

By the time they had narrowed down their choices to a few top contenders, Alex felt a renewed sense of purpose. This was about more than just making money—it was about securing their family's future, about creating something that could last for generations.

As they wrapped up their discussion, Alex turned to Lisa with a smile. "I'm glad we're doing this together. It feels like we're finally on the same page, working towards the same goals."

Lisa smiled back at him, her eyes filled with love and pride. "We've come a long way, haven't we? And I couldn't have done it without you."

They leaned in for a kiss, a moment of quiet connection that spoke volumes about the strength of their relationship. They had weathered the storms together, and now they were building something beautiful—something that would stand the test of time.

As they headed to bed that night, Alex felt a profound sense of peace. The future was full of possibilities, and for the first time in a long time, he felt ready to embrace them all. He had found stability, prosperity, and a sense of purpose that went far beyond financial success. And with Lisa by his side, he knew that whatever challenges lay ahead, they would face them together, with faith, love, and unwavering determination.

As Alex and Lisa continued to move forward with their plans, their lives became increasingly intertwined with the rhythms of their church community. Sundays were no longer just a day of rest, but a time of renewal, a chance to reconnect with their faith and with each other in a deeper way. They had always attended church regularly, but now it felt different—more intentional, more meaningful. Each sermon, each hymn, each prayer resonated with them in ways it hadn't before. The struggles they had endured had opened their hearts in new ways, allowing them to fully absorb the messages of hope, love, and redemption that Pastor John shared each week.

"Alex, Lisa," he greeted them warmly, "I've been meaning to talk to you both. There's a new community service group starting up, focused on outreach and support for families going through tough times. I think you two would be a perfect fit."

Lisa glanced at Alex, her eyes lighting up at the prospect. "That sounds wonderful, Pastor. We've been looking for more ways to get involved, to give back."

Pastor John smiled, clearly pleased by her enthusiasm. "I thought you might be interested. It's a small group, but we're hoping to make a big impact. We'll be helping with everything from food distribution to organizing support for single parents and struggling families. Your experience and empathy could really make a difference."

Alex nodded, feeling a familiar sense of purpose stirring within him. "We'd love to help. It sounds like exactly what we've been looking for."

Over the next few weeks, Alex and Lisa became more deeply involved in the community service group. They attended meetings, helped organize events, and worked alongside other volunteers to support those in need. It was hard work, but it was also incredibly rewarding, and it brought them even closer as a couple.

As they were preparing food packages for a local shelter on a certain day, Alex paused to take in the scene around him. Lisa was chatting with another volunteer, her face lit up with joy as she packed bags of groceries. Nearby, a group of children were helping sort donated clothing, laughing and playing as they worked. There was a sense of camaraderie, of shared purpose, that filled the room with warmth and light. Alex felt a deep sense of gratitude well up inside him. This was what life was all about—serving others, building community, and living out the values of faith and love. He realized that his journey of faith wasn't just about his personal relationship with God, but about how that relationship guided his actions in the world, how it shaped his interactions with others.

As the day came to an end, and they loaded the last of the food packages into a van for delivery, Lisa turned to Alex with a contented sigh.

"This feels so right," she said softly. "I've never felt more connected to my faith, or to you. We're doing something that really matters, something that aligns with everything we believe in."

Alex smiled, pulling her into a gentle embrace. "I feel the same way. It's like everything we've been through has led us to this point, to this place where we can truly live out our faith and make a difference."

Their involvement in the service group became a regular part of their lives, and with each passing week, their faith deepened even further. They prayed together more often, not just for themselves but for the people they were helping, for their community, and for guidance in how best to serve.

Their relationship with God had become a cornerstone of their lives, a source of strength and direction in everything they did. And as they continued to grow in their faith, they found that their love for each other and their sense of purpose only grew stronger.

By the time Christmas rolled around, Alex and Lisa felt a profound sense of fulfillment. The challenges they had faced, the trials and tribulations, had all led them to this point—a place of peace, of service, and of deep, abiding faith. They had built a life together that was rich in love, purpose, and community, and they knew that whatever the future held, they would face it with grace, courage, and unwavering belief in the power of their faith.

The crisp autumn air filtered through the open windows of Alex and Lisa's home, carrying with it the scent of fallen leaves and the promise of new beginnings. It was a Saturday afternoon, and the two of them sat at the dining room table, surrounded by papers and printouts—property listings, mortgage rates, and financial projections.

"This one looks interesting," Lisa said, pointing to a listing for a small duplex on the outskirts of town. "It's not too far from here, and it's in a good neighborhood. The price is reasonable, and with a little work, it could bring in some solid rental income."

Alex leaned in to study the listing. The duplex had two units, each with two bedrooms and a small yard. It wasn't anything fancy, but it was exactly the kind of property they had been looking for— a practical investment that could help secure their financial future.

"I like it," Alex said thoughtfully. "It's not too big of a risk, and it's something we can manage without taking on too much debt. Plus, I think I could handle most of the repairs myself, which would save us some money."

Lisa nodded, her eyes bright with excitement. "I've run the numbers, and if we rent out both units, we could cover the mortgage and still have a little left over each month. It could be a great way to build some additional income, especially as we start thinking about Emma's college expenses and our own retirement."

Alex smiled at the mention of their daughter. Emma was growing up fast, and while she still had a few years before college, the costs were already looming large in their minds. The idea of having an investment property that could help cover those expenses—and maybe even provide a nest egg for the future—was incredibly appealing.

"We've come a long way," Alex mused, leaning back in his chair. "A year ago, I never would have thought we'd be in a position to even consider something like this. But now… it just feels right. Like we're finally taking control of our future."

Lisa reached across the table and took his hand, her touch warm and reassuring. "We've worked hard to get here, and I'm proud of us. This investment isn't just about making money—it's about building something that will last, something that will give us security and peace of mind as we move forward."

They sat in comfortable silence for a few moments, both of them reflecting on how far they had come. The struggles they had faced, the uncertainty and fear, now seemed like distant memories, replaced by a sense of confidence and optimism about the future.

"So, what do you think?" Lisa asked, breaking the silence. "Should we go take a look at it in person?"

Alex smiled, feeling a surge of excitement. "Definitely. Let's call the realtor and set up a time. I want to see it for myself, but I have a good feeling about this."

Over the next few days, Alex and Lisa visited the duplex, walked through the units, and inspected the property. It wasn't perfect—there were a few repairs that needed to be done, and the landscaping was a bit neglected—but overall, it was exactly what they had been looking for.

After discussing their options and weighing the pros and cons, they decided to make an offer. The negotiations went smoothly, and within a few weeks, they found themselves signing the papers and officially becoming owners of their first investment property. As they stood outside the duplex, keys in hand, Alex felt a profound sense of accomplishment. This wasn't just about buying a property—it was about taking another step toward securing their family's future, about building something tangible that would benefit them for years to come.

"We did it," Lisa said, her voice filled with pride as she slipped her arm around Alex's waist. "This is our first big step into the future we've been dreaming about."

Alex smiled, pulling her close. "Yeah, we did. And I couldn't have done it without you."

They spent the rest of the afternoon walking through the property, making plans for the renovations and discussing how they wanted to manage the rentals. It was hard work, but it was work that they were doing together, with a shared vision and a common goal. As the sun began to set, casting a warm glow over the neighborhood, Alex and Lisa locked up the duplex and headed home. They were tired, but it was a good kind of tired—the kind that comes from knowing you're building something real, something that will stand the test of time. Back at home, they settled into their evening routine, but there was a new sense of energy and excitement in the air. The investment property was just the beginning, a tangible symbol of their commitment to each other and to their future. They had faced adversity, rebuilt their lives, and now they were on a path that was filled with hope and promise.

As they climbed into bed that night, Lisa snuggled up next to Alex, resting her head on his shoulder. "I'm so glad we took this step," she murmured. "It feels like we're really building something, like we're creating a legacy for Emma and for ourselves."

Alex kissed the top of her head, his heart full of love and gratitude. "Me too. It's not just about the money—it's about what it represents. We're creating a life that's grounded in faith, family, and a future we can be proud of. And that's something worth working for."

As they drifted off to sleep, Alex couldn't help but think about how much had changed in the past year. The road hadn't been easy, but every challenge, every struggle, had brought them to this moment—a moment of stability, prosperity, and a deep sense of purpose. And as they continued to build their life together, Alex knew that whatever the future held, they would face it with strength, love, and the unshakable belief that they were on the right path.

# CHAPTER 13

Chapter 11: Mentorship

The business continued to thrive, and with it, Alex's sense of purpose deepened. The once small, personal project had grown into something far more significant—an enterprise that not only supported his family but also became a beacon of hope for others in the community.

As his business flourished, Alex found himself reflecting on the journey that had brought him to this point. He remembered the despair and uncertainty, the nights of prayer and doubt, and the gradual rebuilding of his life through faith, perseverance, and the support of those around him. These reflections made him realize that he had an opportunity to give back, to help others who were struggling as he once had.

One day, after a long afternoon of work in his bustling workshop, Alex received an email from Pastor John. The subject line read, "A New Kind of Outreach." Intrigued, Alex opened it and read that Pastor John was looking to start a mentorship program at the church, aimed at helping people who were facing unemployment, financial difficulties, or other challenges similar to what Alex had experienced.

"I've seen how far you've come, Alex," Pastor John wrote. "Your story could inspire others. I'd love for you to be part of this program, to mentor those who are struggling and help them find their way back to stability and faith."

Alex sat back, feeling a deep sense of gratitude and responsibility. He had often thought about how he could make a difference in other people's lives, but this was the first time he'd been given a concrete opportunity to do so. He replied to Pastor John's email almost immediately, expressing his interest and asking for more details.

A week later, Alex found himself sitting in a meeting room at the church, surrounded by a small group of other mentors—some were local business owners like himself, others were professionals with expertise in areas like finance, counseling, and career development. Pastor John led the meeting, explaining the goals of the program and how they planned to support people in the community.

"We're here to be a guiding light for those who've lost their way," Pastor John said. "Whether it's helping someone craft a resume, teaching them how to budget, or simply offering a listening ear, our goal is to lift them up and show them that there is hope and a path forward."

When it was Alex's turn to speak, he shared his story with the group—his layoff, the betrayal he had felt, the spiritual crisis, and ultimately, the steps he took to rebuild his life. As he spoke, he could see how his words resonated with the others, many of whom nodded in understanding.

"I've been where they are," Alex concluded. "And I know how important it is to have someone who believes in you when you can't believe in yourself. If I can be that person for someone else, I want to do it."

The mentorship program launched a few weeks later. Alex was paired with three mentees, each at a different stage in their journey. The first was a young man named Kevin, who had recently lost his job and was struggling to support his family. The second was a woman named Sandra, who was trying to start her own business after years of working in a dead-end job. The third was an older gentleman named Thomas, who had been forced into early retirement and was feeling lost without the structure and purpose that work had provided.

Alex met with each of them individually, listening to their stories, offering advice, and sharing his experiences. He helped Kevin rewrite his resume and practice for interviews. With Sandra, he discussed the challenges of entrepreneurship, sharing the lessons he had learned from starting his own business. With Thomas, he spent time talking about the emotional toll of losing one's career and the importance of finding new ways to contribute and stay engaged.

Over time, Alex saw each of his mentees make progress. Kevin secured a job that not only paid the bills but also gave him a sense of pride. Sandra's business started to gain traction, and she was excited about the future. Thomas found new purpose through volunteering, discovering that he still had much to offer his community.

But it wasn't just the mentees who benefited from the program—Alex found that he was growing as well. The process of mentoring others forced him to reflect on his own journey, to articulate the lessons he had learned and the values he held dear. It deepened his sense of gratitude and reinforced his commitment to living a life of purpose and service.

One day, after a particularly meaningful session with Thomas, Alex returned home to find Lisa and Emma waiting for him in the kitchen. They had prepared a special dinner to celebrate the latest milestone in his business—a partnership with a local retailer that would carry his custom furniture in their stores.

As they sat down to eat, Alex looked around the table at the faces of his family, feeling a profound sense of contentment. The journey had been long and difficult, but it had also been transformative. He had not only rebuilt his life but had also found a way to lift others up along the way.

After dinner, as they were cleaning up, Lisa came over and wrapped her arms around Alex. "I'm so proud of you," she said softly. "You've come so far, and you're making such a difference in people's lives. I know it hasn't been easy, but you've shown all of us what it means to keep faith and keep going."

Alex smiled, holding her close. "I couldn't have done it without you," he replied. "Without you, Emma, and the support of everyone who's been there for us."

Later that night, as he sat down with his Bible, Alex turned to the Psalms, seeking words that would reflect the gratitude and peace he felt. His eyes fell on Psalm 40: "I waited patiently for the Lord; he turned to me and heard my cry. He lifted me out of the slimy pit, out of the mud and mire; he set my feet on a rock and gave me a firm place to stand."

The words resonated deeply with Alex. They captured the essence of his journey—from the depths of despair to the solid ground he now stood on, supported by his faith, his family, and his community.

As he closed the Bible, Alex offered a prayer of thanks—not just for the blessings he had received, but for the opportunity to pass those blessings on to others. He knew that his story wasn't just his own; it was part of a larger narrative of hope, resilience, and the power of faith.

And as he prepared to rest, Alex felt a sense of fulfillment that went beyond any business success or personal achievement. He was living a life of meaning, connected to others, and guided by the values that had seen him through the darkest of times.

As Alex closed the Bible, the weight of his journey settled over him, not as a burden, but as a testament to the resilience of the human spirit and the grace that had carried him through it all. The words of Psalm 40 echoed in his mind, each verse a reminder of how far he had come. He thought about the pit he had once been in, the darkness that had seemed insurmountable, and the countless nights when he had doubted that anything good could come from his struggles.

But here he was, on the other side of that pit, standing on solid ground. It wasn't just the success of his business that gave him this sense of stability—it was the spiritual growth, the deepening of his faith, and the support of those who had walked alongside him, even when the path was rough.

Alex's thoughts drifted back to the early days, when everything had started to fall apart. The layoff had shaken him to his core, unraveling the life he had known and thrusting him into a world of uncertainty. The discovery of Lisa's affair had been another blow, one that had left him questioning everything—his marriage, his faith, and his own worth. He had felt abandoned, not just by those he loved, but by God Himself.

Yet, in those darkest moments, there had been glimmers of hope. He remembered Pastor John's words during their first meeting at the food bank, when Alex had been on the brink of losing everything, including his home. The pastor had spoken of suffering, of faith tested in the crucible of life's hardest trials, and of a God who never abandoned His children, even when they felt most alone.

Those words had sparked something in Alex—a small flame of hope that had refused to be extinguished, no matter how fierce the storm around him had raged. That hope had led him back to church, to the support group where he had found others who understood his pain and shared his doubts. It had been a slow, sometimes painful journey, but step by step, Alex had begun to rebuild—not just his life, but his faith.

As the weeks had turned into months, and months into years, Alex had come to see his struggles not as punishments, but as opportunities for growth. Each challenge had forced him to confront his fears, to lean into his faith, and to rely on the support of his family and community. The spiritual texts he had once read out of obligation became sources of comfort and wisdom. The prayers he had once whispered in desperation became conversations with a God he now knew was listening, guiding him through the darkness toward the light.

His business, born out of necessity, had become more than just a means to an end. It was a reflection of his journey, a testament to his resilience, creativity, and the lessons he had learned along the way. The furniture he crafted with his hands symbolized the life he had rebuilt with his heart—solid, sturdy, and infused with a deeper purpose.

And then there was the mentorship program. It had given Alex a new sense of purpose, one that went beyond personal success. In helping others, he had found healing for himself. Each time he shared his story, he was reminded of how far he had come, and each time he saw a mentee take a step forward, he felt a renewed sense of hope for the future.

Sitting in the quiet of his home, Alex realized that his journey was far from over. There would be more challenges, more opportunities for growth, and more people to help along the way. But for the first time in a long while, he felt truly at peace with where he was and where he was headed.

He thought about the people who had been part of his journey—Lisa, who had stood by him as they rebuilt their marriage; Emma, whose youthful optimism had been a beacon of light during their darkest days; Pastor John, whose guidance had been a lifeline; and Emily, who had helped them navigate the financial storms with wisdom and care. Each of them had played a role in his healing, and for that, Alex was deeply grateful.

He knew he would never have made it this far on his own. It was the support of his loved ones, the community that had embraced him, and the faith that had been reignited within him that had brought him to this place of peace and purpose. As he reflected on all of this, Alex felt a deep sense of humility. He had been given a second chance, not just at life, but at living a life that truly mattered.

Before heading to bed, Alex took one last look out of the window, where the night sky was dotted with stars. Each one seemed to represent a blessing, a lesson, or a person who had touched his life in some way. He smiled, feeling a profound sense of connection to something greater than himself—a divine plan that had guided him through the darkest of nights and brought him to a place where he could now be a light for others.

With a heart full of gratitude and peace, Alex whispered a quiet prayer of thanks, not just for the journey he had walked, but for the strength and faith to keep moving forward, no matter what lay ahead.

# CHAPTER 14

As Alex continued his work with the mentorship program, he began to notice a recurring theme in the stories he heard from those he mentored. Many of them were struggling not just with the practical aspects of unemployment—like finding a new job or managing their finances—but also with the emotional and psychological toll it took on them. The loss of identity, the feelings of isolation, and the erosion of self-worth were common threads in their narratives, and Alex knew from experience how devastating these could be. He also realized that while the church's mentorship program was making a difference, there was a larger need in the community—something that went beyond what the church could provide alone. Alex began to think about how he could expand the reach of the program, to create something more comprehensive that could address the multifaceted challenges faced by unemployed professionals.

One evening, after a particularly meaningful session with his mentees, Alex sat down with Pastor John to discuss his ideas.

"Pastor, I've been thinking," Alex began, "there's so much more we could do for people who are going through what I went through. The mentorship program is a great start, but what if we could create something bigger—something that brings together resources, support, and a sense of community for those who've lost their jobs?"

Pastor John listened intently, nodding as Alex outlined his thoughts. "I think you're onto something, Alex," he said. "We've seen firsthand how much people benefit from having someone to talk to and guide them. But you're right—there are other needs that we could address if we had the right structure in place."

Encouraged by Pastor John's support, Alex spent the next few weeks researching what other communities had done to support unemployed professionals. He looked into career counseling services, job search workshops, financial planning seminars, and even mental health resources. He also reached out to local businesses, community leaders, and other churches to gauge their interest in collaborating on such an initiative. The response was overwhelmingly positive. Many people Alex spoke with had either been affected by unemployment themselves or knew someone who had. They understood the importance of providing not just practical assistance but also emotional and spiritual support to those in need. With this momentum behind him, Alex decided to take the next step. He proposed the creation of a local support network specifically designed for unemployed professionals—a place where they could find not only job search assistance but also a community that understood their struggles.

He presented the idea to the church's leadership team, outlining his vision for the network. It would include:

1. Job Search Assistance: Regular workshops on resume writing, interview techniques, and networking strategies, led by professionals in the field. They would also partner with local businesses to create job fairs and employment opportunities.

2. Financial Planning: Seminars and one-on-one sessions with financial advisors, like Emily, who could help individuals manage their finances during periods of unemployment. This would include budgeting, debt management, and strategies for making the most of limited resources.

3. Emotional and Spiritual Support: Group meetings, similar to the church's support group, where people could share their experiences, offer encouragement, and find solace in their faith. They would also provide access to counseling services for those struggling with anxiety, depression, or other mental health challenges.

4. Skill Development: Partnerships with local educational institutions to offer workshops and courses on skills that were in demand in the job market. This would help individuals stay competitive and increase their chances of finding new employment.

5. Community Building: Regular social events and activities that would foster a sense of belonging and reduce the isolation many unemployed professionals feel. This could include everything from potluck dinners to volunteer opportunities within the community.

The church's leadership team was impressed by Alex's thoroughness and passion. They agreed to provide space for the meetings and workshops and to help promote the network within the congregation and the wider community.

But Alex didn't stop there. He knew that for the network to be truly effective, it needed to be a community-wide effort. He reached out to other churches, local non-profits, and even government agencies, inviting them to join the initiative. He also tapped into his growing network of business contacts, asking them to contribute in whatever ways they could—whether by offering job opportunities, volunteering their time, or providing financial support. The response was even better than Alex had hoped. Within a few months, the local support network for unemployed professionals was up and running. It quickly became a lifeline for many in the community who were struggling to find their way back to stability. Alex was deeply involved in the network from the start, leading workshops, mentoring new members, and using his own story to inspire others. But what made him most proud was seeing how the community came together to support one another. People who had once been isolated by their struggles were now connected, not just by their shared challenges but by a renewed sense of hope and purpose.

One evening, as Alex stood at the back of the room during a particularly well-attended job search workshop, he watched as people he had once mentored were now leading sessions and offering advice to others. He saw the smiles, the handshakes, the looks of determination, and he knew that something special had been created. The local support network wasn't just a place to find a job or get financial advice—it was a community where people could rebuild their lives, supported by others who understood what they were going through. It was a place where faith and perseverance were celebrated, where setbacks were seen as opportunities for growth, and where no one had to walk the journey alone.

As the evening wound down and people began to leave, Alex felt a tap on his shoulder. He turned to see Pastor John standing beside him, a proud smile on his face.

"You've done something remarkable here, Alex," Pastor John said. "This network is changing lives, and it's all because you saw a need and decided to do something about it."

Alex shook his head modestly. "It wasn't just me," he replied. "This was a community effort. And it wouldn't have happened without your support—or without everything I went through to get here."

Pastor John nodded. "True. But it takes someone with vision and courage to turn an idea into reality. And that someone was you."

As they walked out of the church together, Alex felt a deep sense of fulfillment. He had come full circle, from a man who had once been lost and broken to someone who was now helping others find their way. The journey had been long and difficult, but it had also been worth every step. And as he looked out at the night sky, with the stars shining brightly above, Alex knew that this was just the beginning. There were more people to help, more lives to touch, and more ways to make a difference. And he was ready to continue that work, guided by the faith, hope, and love that had brought him this far.

# CHAPTER 15

The day dawned bright and clear, with the first rays of sunlight streaming through the windows of Alex and Lisa's home. There was an air of excitement and anticipation in the house, as today marked not one, but two significant milestones for their family. It was the anniversary of Alex's business—a small venture that had grown into a thriving enterprise—and it was also Emma's high school graduation day. As Alex stood in the kitchen, preparing breakfast, he reflected on how far they had come. The sounds of sizzling bacon and the aroma of freshly brewed coffee filled the air, mingling with the memories of countless mornings just like this one, yet so very different. There had been a time when the future felt uncertain, when every day seemed like a battle to hold onto hope. But today, as he flipped the pancakes and set the table, there was a sense of peace that had been hard-won.

Lisa entered the kitchen, a smile lighting up her face as she saw Alex at the stove. She wrapped her arms around him from behind, resting her chin on his shoulder.

"Big day," she said softly, her voice full of warmth.

"Big day," Alex echoed, turning his head to kiss her on the cheek. "Hard to believe, isn't it?"

Lisa nodded, her eyes misting over with emotion. "We've come a long way."

They shared a quiet moment, both lost in their thoughts. For Lisa, it had been a journey of rebuilding trust and reconnecting with the man she loved. For Alex, it had been a path of rediscovery—of himself, his faith, and his purpose. Together, they had weathered the storms, and now, they stood stronger than ever.

Emma bounded into the kitchen, her cap and gown in hand, her excitement barely contained. "Mom, Dad, can you believe it? I'm graduating today!"

Alex grinned, feeling a surge of pride as he looked at his daughter. "We can believe it, Em. You've worked hard for this."

Lisa reached out to smooth a stray lock of hair from Emma's face. "You're going to do amazing things, sweetheart. We're so proud of you."

The three of them sat down to breakfast, the conversation lively as they talked about the day ahead. There would be a ceremony at the school, followed by a celebration at home with close friends and family. And later, they would head to the workshop, where Alex had a special surprise planned for the anniversary of his business.

The graduation ceremony was a blur of caps, gowns, and applause. As Emma walked across the stage to receive her diploma, Alex felt a lump rise in his throat. This was a moment he had dreamed of, even in the darkest times, and seeing it come to fruition was overwhelming. As Emma turned to face the crowd, her eyes searching for her parents, Alex and Lisa stood, clapping and cheering, their hearts full. After the ceremony, they gathered with friends and family at their home. The house was filled with laughter and the sounds of celebration, the warmth of their community palpable. It was a far cry from the days when Alex had isolated himself, afraid to face the world. Now, their home was a place of love and connection, a testament to the healing power of faith and perseverance.

Later in the afternoon, as the sun began to dip in the sky, Alex led Lisa and Emma to his workshop. The space was more than just a place where he crafted furniture—it was a sanctuary, a symbol of his journey from despair to purpose.

"Close your eyes," Alex instructed as they stood at the door.

Lisa and Emma exchanged curious glances but did as they were told. Alex opened the door, guiding them inside before allowing them to look.

"Okay, open them," he said, his voice filled with anticipation.

When they did, they gasped in unison. There, in the center of the workshop, was a beautifully crafted wooden plaque. It was engraved with the words, "Hope Restored," surrounded by intricate carvings of vines and leaves—symbols of growth, renewal, and the enduring strength of their family.

"I wanted something to mark this anniversary," Alex explained, his voice thick with emotion. "Something that represents everything we've been through and everything we've built together. This business, our family, our lives… it's all a testament to hope."

Lisa stepped forward, tears brimming in her eyes as she traced the carvings with her fingers. "It's beautiful, Alex. Just like everything you've made here."

Emma beamed with pride. "This is incredible, Dad. I always knew you were talented, but this… this is something else."

Alex smiled, his heart swelling with love for his family. "It's not just my work—it's ours. Everything I've done, I've done because of you two."

As they stood there, the three of them together, surrounded by the fruits of Alex's labor, there was a sense of closure—of one chapter ending and another beginning. The struggles of the past were behind them, and the future stretched out before them, filled with promise.

The rest of the evening was spent in the warmth of their home, surrounded by friends and family who had supported them through thick and thin. They toasted to Emma's bright future and to the success of Alex's business. But more than anything, they celebrated the journey—the ups and downs, the challenges and triumphs, and the faith that had seen them through it all. As the night drew to a close and the last guests departed, Alex found himself standing on the porch, gazing out at the stars. It was quiet now, the kind of peaceful silence that only comes after a day well spent. He felt Lisa's presence beside him as she slipped her hand into his.

"Everything okay?" she asked, her voice soft.

Alex nodded, his eyes still on the sky. "More than okay. I was just thinking about everything… about how grateful I am."

Lisa leaned her head against his shoulder. "We've been blessed, haven't we?"

"We have," Alex agreed. "And I'm ready for whatever comes next. Whatever challenges or opportunities are ahead, I know we can face them together."

They stood there for a while, simply enjoying the moment, the quiet, and each other's company. The journey had been long and often difficult, but it had brought them to a place of peace, love, and a deep understanding of what truly mattered.

As they turned to go inside, Alex looked back one last time at the stars, a sense of anticipation rising within him. The future was a mystery, but it was one he was eager to embrace, with his family by his side and his faith as his guide. It was a new chapter, and for the first time in a long while, Alex felt ready—ready to write it, ready to live it, and ready to face whatever it would bring with hope, strength, and unwavering gratitude.

As the weeks passed, life began to settle into a new rhythm for Alex and Lisa. The intensity of the past few years had given way to a quieter, more contented existence. Emma was preparing for college, excited about the next chapter of her life, while Alex's business continued to thrive. They found themselves with more time to enjoy the simple pleasures—morning walks through the park, quiet dinners at home, and evenings spent talking about their hopes and dreams for the future.

One crisp autumn morning, as they strolled through the park hand in hand, Lisa turned to Alex, her eyes sparkling with the warmth of the sun. "You know," she began, "I've been thinking a lot about what's next for us. We've come so far, and I feel like there's still so much we can do—together."

Alex smiled, squeezing her hand gently. "I've been thinking about that too. I feel like we've been given a second chance, not just to live our lives, but to live them with purpose. We've been through so much, and it's made us stronger. Now, it's about what we do with that strength."

Lisa nodded, her expression thoughtful. "Maybe we could start something new—a project, or a cause that we're passionate about. Something that gives back, that makes a difference."

"I like that idea," Alex agreed. "Maybe we could even tie it into the support network. There are so many people out there who need help, who need someone to believe in them. We could use our experiences to inspire and support others, just like we've been supported."

As they walked, the conversation flowed easily between them, ideas blossoming like the colorful leaves that surrounded them. They talked about starting a foundation to help unemployed professionals and their families, creating more opportunities for mentorship, and perhaps even organizing community events that would bring people together. The possibilities seemed endless, and for the first time in a long time, the future felt not just hopeful, but bright with potential.

But there was still one more thing that Alex felt he needed to do before fully embracing this new chapter in their lives. It had been on his mind for some time—a lingering desire to have one final, deep conversation with Pastor John. He wanted to talk about everything he had learned, everything he had struggled with, and most importantly, his relationship with God. A few days later, Alex found himself sitting in Pastor John's office at the church, the familiar surroundings comforting yet charged with significance. The pastor greeted him warmly, sensing that this conversation was different from the others they had shared.

"Alex, it's always good to see you," Pastor John said, taking a seat across from him. "What's on your mind?"

Alex took a deep breath, gathering his thoughts. "Pastor, I've been thinking a lot about everything that's happened—about my journey, my faith, and my relationship with God. I've learned so much, but I still have questions, and I guess I just wanted to talk them through with you."

Pastor John nodded, his expression open and inviting. "I'm glad you came to me, Alex. Life is full of questions, and our faith is what helps us navigate them. What's been weighing on your heart?"

Alex paused, searching for the right words. "I guess I've been reflecting on how much I've changed over the past few years—how my faith has been tested, broken down, and then rebuilt. There were times when I felt completely abandoned, like God had turned His back on me. But now, looking back, I can see how those moments of despair were part of a bigger picture—part of something that was meant to shape me, even when I couldn't see it."

Pastor John listened intently, his gaze never leaving Alex's face. "It's true that our hardest trials often lead to the greatest growth. But that doesn't make them any easier to endure when we're in the middle of them. What you're describing is something many people go through—a dark night of the soul, where God feels distant, and we're left to grapple with our doubts and fears."

Alex nodded slowly. "That's exactly it. I felt so lost, so angry. But then, piece by piece, I started to see how those experiences were drawing me closer to God, not pushing me away. It's almost like I had to be broken down completely so that I could be rebuilt— stronger, more resilient, and more connected to my faith."

Pastor John smiled gently. "God works in mysterious ways, Alex. Sometimes, He allows us to go through hardship not to punish us, but to refine us—to strip away the things that are holding us back and to bring us closer to Him. It's like the process of refining silver—the metal has to be heated until all the impurities rise to the surface and are removed, leaving behind something pure and valuable."

Alex absorbed Pastor John's words, feeling a deep resonance within him. "I think I understand that now. But it's also made me realize how important it is to stay connected to God, even when things are going well. I don't want to forget what I've learned or let my faith slip just because life has become easier."

"That's a wise insight, Alex," Pastor John said. "It's easy to turn to God when we're in need, but maintaining that connection during times of peace and prosperity requires conscious effort. It's about cultivating a relationship with God that's not just based on what He can do for us, but on who He is to us. It's about seeking Him in the everyday moments, in the quiet spaces of our lives, and in the decisions we make moving forward."

Alex felt a deep sense of clarity as he listened. "I want to keep growing, Pastor. I want to live my life with intention, guided by my faith. And I want to help others do the same—to be a source of support and encouragement for those who are struggling, just like you were for me."

Pastor John's eyes shone with pride. "You're already doing that, Alex. Your journey, your story, is a powerful testimony to God's grace and the strength of the human spirit. By sharing it with others, you're not only helping them find their way, but you're also continuing to grow in your own faith."

The two men sat in silence for a moment, the weight of their conversation settling into the room like a gentle, comforting presence. It was a silence filled with understanding, with the acknowledgment of the struggles that had been faced and the victories that had been won.

Finally, Alex spoke again, his voice steady and sure. "I'm ready to move forward, Pastor. Whatever comes next, I'm ready to face it with faith, with resilience, and with the knowledge that I'm not alone. God has been with me every step of the way, even when I couldn't see Him, and I know He'll continue to guide me as I step into this new chapter."

Pastor John reached across the table, placing a hand on Alex's shoulder. "You've come a long way, Alex, and I have no doubt that God has great things in store for you. Keep your heart open, keep your faith strong, and remember that you're never alone in this journey. And whenever you need to talk, you know where to find me."

Alex smiled, feeling a profound sense of peace. "Thank you, Pastor. For everything."

As he left the church and stepped out into the crisp autumn air, Alex felt lighter, as if a burden had been lifted from his shoulders. He had found the closure he needed, the answers he had been searching for, and the strength to continue moving forward. He knew that life would still have its challenges, but he was no longer afraid. He had faith, he had purpose, and he had a community of people who loved and supported him. And most importantly, he had a deep, unshakable connection to God, who had seen him through the darkest times and brought him into the light. With a renewed sense of purpose, Alex headed home, ready to share the day with Lisa and Emma, ready to embrace the future with open arms. It was a new chapter, and he was eager to see where it would lead. Whatever came next, he knew they would face it together, with faith, resilience, and the unwavering belief that the best was yet to come.

The evening sky was painted with shades of violet and deep indigo, the last remnants of daylight clinging to the horizon. A gentle breeze rustled through the trees, carrying the scent of freshly cut grass and blooming flowers. Alex stood on the porch of his new home, the wood beneath his feet warm from the day's sun, and watched as the first stars began to twinkle overhead. Inside, the sounds of laughter and conversation drifted out through the open windows. Friends and family had gathered to celebrate Emma's high school graduation and the first anniversary of Alex's business. The house was filled with warmth and joy, the kind of atmosphere that only comes from hard-won happiness. But for a moment, Alex needed a breath of fresh air, a quiet moment to himself to reflect on everything that had led him to this point. He stepped off the porch and wandered down the path that led to the small, serene pond at the edge of the property. The water's surface was calm, reflecting the moonlight in ripples that seemed to dance with the night.

As he reached the edge of the pond, he felt a presence beside him. He looked up to see Lisa, her smile soft and knowing, as if she had sensed he needed her by his side.

"It's beautiful out here," she said, her voice barely above a whisper.

"It is," Alex agreed, slipping his arm around her waist. They stood there together, the cool night air wrapping around them like a gentle embrace.

"I'm so proud of Emma," Lisa continued, leaning her head against Alex's shoulder. "And I'm proud of you too, Alex. And us, for the most part. Just take a look at how far we've come."

Alex nodded, his heart swelling with emotion. "We've been through a lot, haven't we?"

Lisa chuckled softly. "That's an understatement. We've been through hell, and then some. But we made it. We're stronger, and we've got so much to look forward to."

They fell into a comfortable silence, each lost in their thoughts, savoring the peacefulness of the moment. But as Alex stared out over the pond, a thought began to form in his mind—something he had never really considered before but that now seemed to make perfect sense.

"Hey babe," he began slowly, his voice tinged with excitement, "what if we took this a step further? What if we made a real, lasting difference in this community?"

Lisa looked up at him, curiosity in her eyes. "What do you mean?" She didn't reveal even the slightest bit of excitement at what he had called her. But she was going crazy on the inside.

"I mean," Alex said, turning to face her fully, "so, and I'm just spitballing here, what if we bought some more land? Maybe like a large piece of land, and created a retreat center from it? A place where people who are going through what we went through can come to heal, to find peace and direction. Well, that was already part of the plan but we could also offer workshops, counseling, spiritual guidance, and a chance to reconnect with nature. It could be a sanctuary for those who need a fresh start. Hell, bump it up into some kind of semi-gaming arena for our nerds out there, give 'em something that feels a little like home, you know?"

Lisa's eyes widened as the idea took root in her mind. "Alex, that's... that's incredible. I love it. We could even bring in other professionals—therapists, career coaches, pastors—to help guide people through their journeys."

"Exactly," Alex said, feeling a surge of energy as the vision became clearer. "We've been so blessed, and I think it's our turn to give back in a big way. This could be our legacy—a place where people can come to rediscover themselves and their purpose."

Lisa smiled, a radiant smile that mirrored the stars above. "I think it's perfect. Let's do it."

They embraced, the excitement and possibility of this new venture electrifying the air around them. It was as if everything they had been through—every trial, every heartbreak, every moment of doubt—had been leading them to this.

As they walked back toward the house, hand in hand, they talked about the plans, the possibilities, the people they would help. The idea felt right, felt big, felt like the culmination of everything they had learned and experienced.

But just as they reached the porch, the sounds of music began to drift out from the house. Someone had turned on the stereo, and a familiar song—a song from their early days together—began to play. Without a word, Alex turned to Lisa, a mischievous smile on his face.

"May I have this dance, m'lady?" he asked, bowing slightly in mock formality.

Lisa laughed, a joyful, unguarded sound, and curtsied in return. "I'd be honored."

They began to dance under the open sky, the moonlight casting their shadows across the lawn. The music, the laughter, the sound of their feet moving in time to the rhythm—it was as if the universe itself had paused to watch this moment, this celebration of life, love, and the future. As they swayed to the music, lost in each other and in the moment, the world around them seemed to fade away. It was just the two of them, dancing through life, ready to face whatever came next with the same faith, resilience, and love that had brought them this far. And in that dance, in that perfect, out-of-the-box moment, Alex knew that this was only the beginning. The future was wide open, full of possibilities, and they were ready— together—to embrace it all.

**Other Books by the Author**

1. Tangled Hearts

2. Silent Vision

3. Silent Vision 2 Codename Echo

4. Man up

5. Woman up

6. Couple up

7. Marriage is it worth the fight?

8. Sheltered Hearts

9. Empowering the Future: a guide to raising strong and resilient Black Children

10. WYGDN What You Gonna Do Now

All books are available on https://www.faithharbourbooks.com/